Teaching Children
Responsibility

Teaching Children Responsibility

Linda and Richard Eyre

Photography by the authors

Deseret Book Company
Salt Lake City, Utah

©1982 Deseret Book Company

All rights reserved. No part of this book may be reproduced in any form or by any means without permission in writing from the publisher, Deseret Book Company, P.O. Box 30178, Salt Lake City, Utah 84130.

Deseret Book is a registered trademark of Deseret Book Company.

ISBN 0-87579-318-5

Printed in the United States of America

CONTENTS

	Preface	vii
	Acknowledgments	viii
1	To You as a Parent	2
2	More Than Putting Away Pajamas	8
3	How to Use This Book	16

Section I	RESPONSIBILITY TO PARENTS (OBEDIENCE)	23
4	Responsibility for Obedience	26
5	Responsibility for Things	44
6	Responsibility for Work	60

Section II	RESPONSIBILITY TO GOD (STEWARDSHIP)	77
7	Responsibility for Actions	84
8	Responsibility for Gifts	102
9	Responsibility for the Holy Ghost	116

Section III	RESPONSIBILITY TO SELF (DISCIPLINE)	135
10	Responsibility for Choices	140
11	Responsibility for Character	156
12	Responsibility for Potential	174

Section IV	RESPONSIBILITY TO OTHERS (SERVICE)	195
13	Responsibility for Smaller Children	198
14	Responsibility for Dependability	210
15	Responsibility for Contributing	224
	Index	243

PREFACE

We write together, but we write differently. He writes conceptually, sequentially, step by step; she writes emotionally, incidentally, thought by thought—two ways to think about the same ideas. In this book his writing is in regular print, *hers is in italics.*

It is important to us that you realize that all the content is ours together. The concepts came in discussion. He wrote more of it than she because his business schedule offered a little more time than her homemaking schedule. (It's easier to write on an airplane or in an office waiting for a meeting than in the middle of fixing lunches or in the laundry room waiting for the dryer.)

So the thinking was done together and the writing down was done separately. We hope you who are married will take things out of the book the same way we put them in—reading them separately, thinking about them and implementing them together.

ACKNOWLEDGMENTS

Special gratitude to:

Members of TCJ parents' groups throughout the country who have put our previous book *Teaching Children Joy* into full effect and spawned many of the ideas for *Teaching Children Responsibility*.

Corry DeMille, typist and "unscrambler" par excellence, who is also the capable manager of the TCJ parent group system.

Both extensions of our "tree trunk"—the "roots" (our parents), who provided the nourishment and the connection to earth, and the "branches" (our children), who send down the sunshine and cause us to care.

Teaching Children
Responsibility

To You as a Parent 1

Maybe you've felt it too.

It was a month or so after our second child had been born. Our oldest one was nearly two. We were feeling the fear that comes from *being* parents before one has learned *how* to be a parent.

We could already see how different this second little child was from the first, and the frightful thought occurred that all our hard-learned, trial-and-error lessons on how to handle the first wouldn't work at all on the second. We realized we were beginner parents in an advanced class. We had gone to school fifteen or twenty years to learn the concepts and skills necessary for our professions, but we didn't have a single credit-hour toward parenting.

Because I had just emerged from graduate school, I took a student's approach to parenting. I responded to my fears by going to the nearest bookstore. I bought eleven paperback books on parenting and brought them home. I spread them out on the table and began to study.

What a shock to discover that none of them agreed on anything! Just when I had been convinced by one author's view on discipline, another author argued so compellingly for an opposite theory that I changed my mind. The credentials and degrees of the writers didn't lead to similar views at all. They simply gave them license to disagree very convincingly.

We responded to their disagreements by throwing all the books away. We adopted an opposite approach. Since the so-called experts and all their expertise produced no consensus, we decided to disregard all expertise and adopt the simplest view of all: namely, that techniques and theories don't even matter—that the whole key is *love*. We would simply love our children with all our hearts, and everything else would take care of itself.

That notion lasted only until we realized how much evidence there was against it. My business partner and his wife, we observed, loved their daughter and showed it by giving her everything she wanted. The result of their love was an insufferably spoiled and unhappy child. A neighbor of ours loved his son and showed it by spending every spare moment trying to make him into the ballplayer he had always wanted his son to be. The result of his love was a nervous, erratic child who was making neither himself nor his father happy.

It occurred to us that love must be intelligent rather than indulgent, that love that is unintelligently applied can be harmful. We realized once again that we needed at least a basic philosophy for parenting, a set of parental goals and some notions of how to achieve them, a framework within which to apply our love.

Our concern and fear were based not only on the love we felt for those two little children and our desire to do right by them, but also on our belief: in a purpose and plan of life; in a Heavenly Father who, until this life had been the only parent but who now had given us his role and stewardship over others of his children; in his promise that if we handled the parenting role well, we could keep it for eternity.

Our *love* and our *belief* scared us, made parenthood seem overwhelming in its importance, and drove us to a quest for a personal philosophy of parenting.

Initially our quest was built around the question "What do we want for our children?" It seemed like the right question. We would simply base how we handled our children and what we tried to give them on the things we wanted them to have. The trouble was, there were so many things; security, confidence, creativity, friendliness, peace of mind, imagination, self-esteem, concern for others, a sense of service. The list kept getting longer. What we were developing was a wish-list rather than a workable philosophy.

The breakthrough occurred when we changed the question. We realized that we were only surrogate parents, that the real parent was God, and the real question was not what *we* want for our children, but what *He* wants for them.

Now we were getting somewhere. There were *answers* for the question "What does God want for his children in mortality?"—profound and simple scriptural answers.

What we were really asking was, "What are the purposes of mortality, and how can we help our children (His children) accomplish those purposes?" We searched the scriptures and eventually boiled the answers down to three:

1. *We should teach our children joy.* "Men are that they might have joy." In the gospel sense, there are many kinds and many levels of joy. Children can be taught awareness of all kinds of joy that God sent them here to experience and to find.

2. *We should teach our children responsibility.* Mortality is a test of our willingness and ability to work out our own salvation, to become responsible agents unto ourselves and to God, thus to be more like him when we return to him. Children who learn responsibility have highly increased chances of doing so.

3. *We should teach our children charity.* Our ultimate objective is to become Christlike; and charity is the pure love of Christ. If children learn the principles of charity from their earthly parents, then Heavenly Father's objective will be realized.

So the three purposes for mortality—joy, responsibility, charity—become the three objectives of parenting. Between them, they provide a framework that includes a place for all principles children should learn.

Further study (and practical application, for the two children who kindled our concern have been joined by five others) led us to feel that the three objectives should be pursued in *sequence.*

Age 0– 6 *Teach children joy*
Age 4–12 *Teach children responsibility*
Age 10–16 *Teach children charity*

There are overlaps. There are elements of responsibility within joy and of charity within responsibility, but busy parents need a focus, a clear, strong, single goal to work on for each phase of a child's growth.

Our book *Teaching Children Joy* was published first. In addition to whatever help it has been to individual parents, it has spawned the formation of hundreds of "TCJ-parents' groups," which conduct "do it yourself" preschools* with curriculums based on the fifteen "joys" in the book.

This volume, *Teaching Children Responsibility*, picks up where that book leaves off. Readers familiar with *Teaching Children Joy* will notice that specific "responsibilities" are extensions of specific "joys." For example, the joy of the earth becomes the responsibility for preserving nature. The joy of individual confidence and uniqueness becomes the responsibility for developing one's gifts and realizing one's potential. The parallels are appropriate because of the connections (for children *and* adults) between joy and responsibility. When responsibility is accepted and carried through, a higher form of joy results.

The third book in the series, *Teaching Children Charity*, will follow.

Together the books provide an active strategy for assisting God's children in finding and achieving the purposes of their mortal probation. They are not a collection of passive philosophies or theories. They are actual blueprints for turning a family into an effective teaching institution.

Most parenting books offer techniques and approaches that are essentially suggestions on how to *react* to children. This book, along with the one that precedes and the one that follows, suggests *actions* rather than *reactions*. They can do so for one reason. They are based not on our ideas of what children should be taught, but on what their true Father (and ours) has said they should learn.

Parents who assist their children in building joy, responsibility, and charity give an eternal gift, for children grow to be parents and pass on the gifts they have been given.

And we will wake to discover that it is not good children we have been raising, but good parents.

---

*For more information about TCJ "Joy Schools" write TCJ, 1775 Yalecrest Avenue, Salt Lake City, Utah 84105. Phone 801-581-0112.

More Than Putting Away Pajamas 2

What does it mean to teach a child responsibility? If you were to ask ten parents, you would probably receive ten different answers. To one it might mean teaching a child to make his bed and put his pajamas away. To another it might involve motivating children to do a family job. Some parents may want to teach children responsibility simply because it would lessen their own work load, giving them more time and more freedom.

In the context of this book, *responsibility* means more than any of these—far more. It means *to become responsible*. It means to become mature in the sense of being responsible *to* family, *to* self, *to* God. It means being responsible *for* all the stewardships of mortality: for our gifts and talents, for our potential, for our affections, for our thoughts, for our actions, for our foreordinations.

Mortality is a test. The essence of the test is whether we can become responsible enough to make the right choices, responsible enough to work out our own salvation.

Responsibility is not the result of maturity, but the cause of it. The responsibility of parents is to teach responsibility.

On its most basic level, responsibility is obedience. At its next higher level, it becomes stewardship, then discipline, then service.

Children best learn responsibility through this sequence. They learn first to be responsible to their parents (obedience); then to be responsible to their heavenly parent (stewardship); then to be responsible to self (discipline); and finally to be responsible to their family and to the human family (service).

Small children can grasp responsibility as it applies to *things*. As they grow, they can become responsible for *work*, for their *actions*, then for their *gifts* and their *potential*, and finally for other *people*, for their brothers and sisters.

The earlier levels of responsibility prepare a child to accept the later levels. The sequence of responsibility can best be understood in diagram form:

Age	Responsibility as	Responsibility for	Responsibility to
4 or younger			
6	obedience	obedience things work	parents
8	stewardship	actions gifts Holy Ghost	Heavenly Father
10	discipline	choices character potential	self
12	service	family dependability contribution	others

Attempting to teach responsibility out of sequence hardly ever succeeds. It is difficult for a child to feel responsible to God at baptism age if he has not previously learned responsibility to his earthly parents. A child usually cannot understand responsibility for his gifts or potential until he has accepted responsibility for his actions and for his things. The concept of stewardship comes much easier to a child who understands obedience.

The pattern of this book follows the pattern of the preceding chart. Section I deals with responsibility to parents, helping children to accept responsibility for their things and then their actions in the context of obedience. Section II builds on the first by helping children see that they have another parent to whom they are responsible, one who has given them everything over which they are stewards. Section III deals with responsibility to self, with discipline and the handling of one's possibilities and potential. Section IV is designed to help parents show children that we are all responsible for each other, that we are our brother's keeper, that our ultimate responsibility is Christlike service.

The ages on the chart and in the sections are general and approximate. We know that the age of accountability and of actual responsibility to God is eight. We know that, prior to baptism, children should gain certain forms of responsibility, particularly to their parents. We know that, as children mature, they become capable of understanding the self-discipline and service that are involved with responsibility. But different children can grasp and gain different forms of responsibility at different ages. What is important is not the precise age, but the *sequence* in which responsibility levels are taught. The concepts of the earlier chapters should be taught to children as early as they can handle them, and should be followed by the succeeding sections in sequence.

So much for theory. Starting with chapter four, this book becomes a method book. Each chapter begins with an illustration and definition of the particular form of responsibility being dealt with and is followed by a list of methods from which parents can pick and choose. Each chapter ends with some particularly effective practices that are called "family focal points" and that should become consistent, ongoing habits within a family to instill and preserve that form of responsibility within the children.

In each chapter, the opening illustration is like a case study, a typical, true-to-life situation that may seem familiar to you. The methods part is essentially a list of ways to teach that form of responsibility. The methods for younger children (starting with age four) are always first in the list, and those designed more for older children (to age twelve) are last. The final part of each chapter is more personal, a particular idea or two from our own family that we think might help other families keep a particular form of responsibility alive and well over the months and years ahead. You will notice that the methods section of each chapter is composed of games, songs, stories, and other activities that teach children the concept of a certain form of responsibility, and that are used only when you are concentrating on the kind of responsibility covered by that particular chapter. The "family focal points," on the other hand, are practices or patterns (in some cases even traditions) that you may want to make permanent and habitual in your family.

In order to understand the basic principles of teaching responsibility to children, we have found that it is crucial to acknowledge and understand four important variables:

1. The child. *Nothing is more evident to us as we raise our children than the fact that each one is unique and different from the others. Just as each one responds to discipline differently, so will each respond to responsibility differently. Although some things must be done uniformly, we should remember that there are different ways to do most things and different ways to help children become responsible. A good exercise mentally and physically is to work out methods on certain responsibilities that work well with each child. If we can help them with "their way" while they are small, it becomes safer to allow them the flexibility to try their own way as they get older.*

2. Our expectations. *One amusing thing that we keep learning over and over about teaching responsibility is that children do exactly what is really expected of them. (And they can tell if you're faking it.)*

One mother I know who had plenty of money to hire household help felt that her children, especially her girls, would be making beds and doing dishes for the rest of their lives once they were married. Since they could afford it, she had decided that now was the time to let them spend their time with skiing, sewing, tennis, and piano lessons while a maid did the work around the house. Though I disagree, the point is that those girls did exactly what was expected of them as far as household responsibilities were concerned—exactly nothing.

3. Example. *A very important tool in teaching children re-*

sponsibility of any kind is example. Children are much less likely to keep their rooms clean if the kitchen is always a disaster and the family room a jumbled mess. If father always leaves his socks wherever they drop, waits for mother to hang up his suit, and never seems to get to the leaky faucet and broken screens, the children will take note.

Once in a while we need to step back and look at ourselves. If we are trying to teach our children something we never learned, maybe our first step is to change ourselves.

4. Consistency and follow-through. *This is a very important variable and without a doubt the hardest part of teaching responsibility.* When our firstborn child was laid in my arms, I remember looking into those baby eyes and daydreaming about a lovely ten-year-old who would come into my room dressed and ready for piano practice at 6:30 A.M. I fancied that she would leave her room clean and tidy and eat a good breakfast before school, return from school, and go straight to her homework and afternoon responsibilities. I suppose that if that little baby had realized what would be expected of her she would have been amazed—but it would not have compared with the shock I would have undergone if I had realized what was required of me in order to make that dream come true.

It's so easy and logical to say, "Now Josh, go clean your room so that you can go to the store with us." But it is not *easy* when you realize that time is short and you've got to get to the store and back, prepare dinner, find a babysitter and leave for the evening. It's even harder to leave him home when you find that his room is still a mess, even knowing that it's his best friend's birthday party and he desperately wants to buy the present himself. But learn he must, and if you take him to the store before he cleans that room, the message is clear: "Mom doesn't really mean it."

We have to be pretty tough-skinned at times in order to be consistent. *The sooner we realize that the amount of responsibility our children learn depends on our consistency and follow-through, no matter how difficult it may be, the better off we are. There is nothing more challenging in terms of patience, understanding, and courage.*

Please realize as you begin to read (as we did when we started to write) that thoughtful, individual handling of each child, of expectations, of example, and of consistency are the keys to success in teaching children responsibility.

How to Use This Book 3

By design, *Teaching Children Responsibility* is more of a program-to-be-used than it is a book-to-be-read. Parents lead complex lives, with various interests and responsibilities tugging at them from all sides. Too often parenting is a low mental priority. We pay it lip service. We know, theoretically, how important it is, but we often do it by reaction, situation by situation, without any real strategy or plan.

Teaching Children Responsibility is a program that, when followed, brings measurable, noticeable, wonderful results. But it is not easy, and it cannot be done subconsciously. It's not a question, in other words, of whether you agree with the theories of the book, but a question of whether you take the time and make the effort to put the book into practice with your own children, of whether you take the responsibility of teaching responsibility.

There are two ways to use the book. The first is simply to try to teach each of your children the kind of responsibility that is most appropriate to their own age (i.e., concentrate on responsibility for "obedience," "things," and "work" with your five-year-old and on responsibility for "choices" and "potential" with your ten-year-old). This approach is probably the simplest if you have only one or two children. On the other hand, if you have several, it will become rather complicated to try to concentrate, at the same time, on many different types of responsibility for many different children. Also, you may have a ten-year-old who has not yet grasped the responsibilities for "things" or for "work."

The alternate approach is to focus as a family on one separate responsibility (one chapter) each month. There are twelve chapters, one for each month of the year. Each chapter has a range of methods for teaching that particular form of responsibility, and the methods are arranged according to how basic they are. The first ones listed in each chapter are for younger children, the last ones for older children. Keep in mind that the ages covered by the book are approximately four to twelve. Thus in each chapter the first methods listed are aimed at four- and five-year-olds, the latter ones at eleven- and twelve-year-olds. Thus, in a given month you could concentrate on a given form of responsibility, choosing the methods and practices most appropriate for the age of each of your children.

In a month when you are concentrating on an "early" responsibility (i.e. responsibility for things), you might work hardest with your younger children, involving the older ones in the teaching and the example setting. In a month when you work on a more advanced responsibility (i.e., responsibility for contribution), you might concentrate principally on your older children and involve the younger ones with only the most basic methods and stories included in that chapter.

If you choose the one-form-of-responsibility-per-month approach, remember that your family's efforts should be cumulative. The major patterns you develop in April while working on the responsibility for actions should be well enough implanted that they continue to function somewhat automatically during May when you shift your conscious efforts to the responsibility for gifts.

Some forms of responsibility fit particularly well with a certain season of the year. For example, "Responsibility for Contributing" fits well with December and the Christmas season.

The "family focal point" in each chapter is specifically intended to become a permanent habit to bring about the desired cumulative effect of continuing beyond the month that a certain responsibility is taught.

When you have followed the program for a full year, start over. The children are now a year older. They have a year's experience. They (and you) can now understand each particular form of responsibility more clearly and develop it more thoroughly.

As you read the "family focal points," please forgive us for using our own children as the illustrations. Also, please do not assume that our children have mastered these concepts or that we are brilliantly or completely successful in implementing the ideas as parents. Many of the ideas are not even ours. We have garnered them from other families. We are in the same boat we hope you are in—we are parents who want to become better parents.

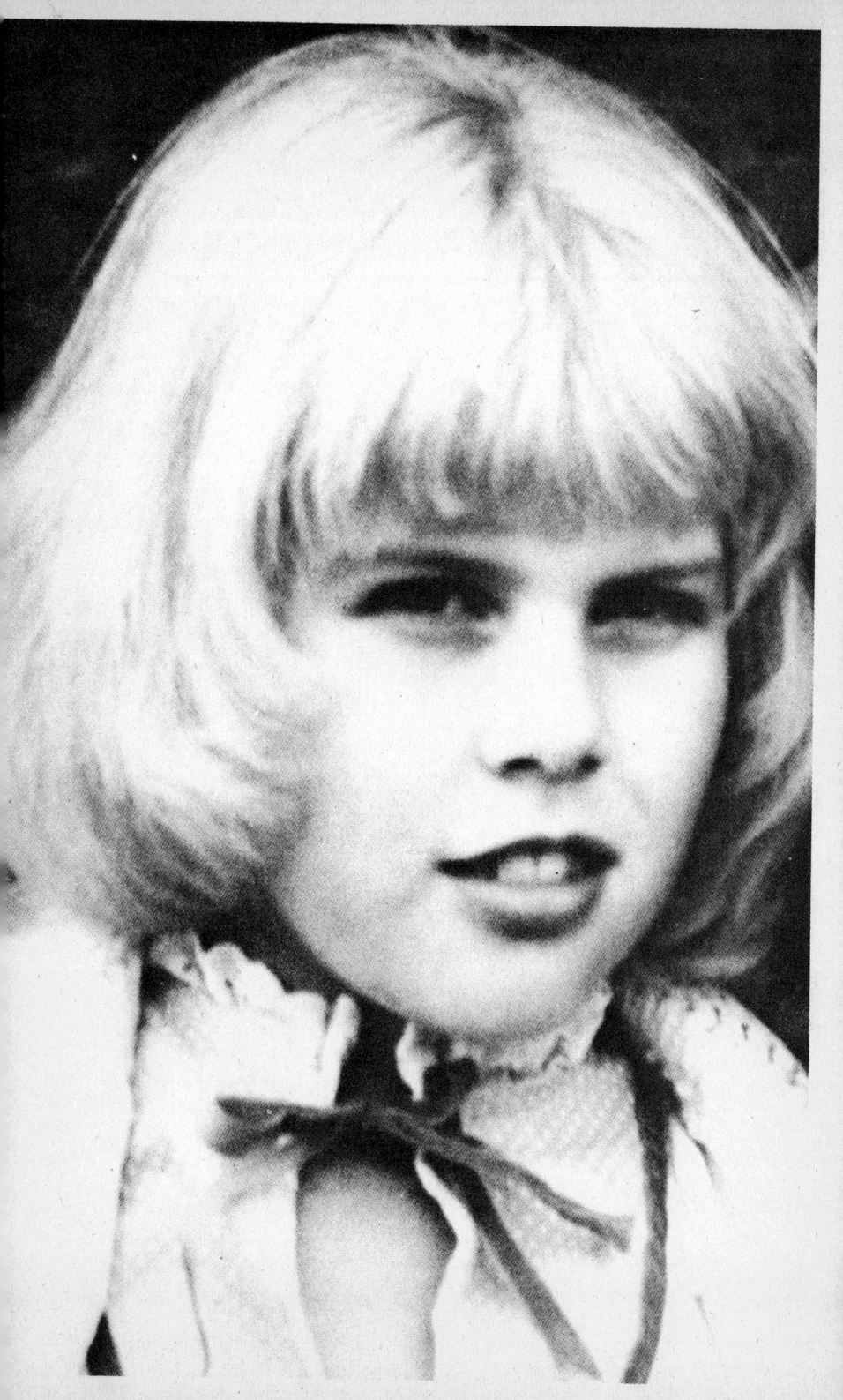

SECTION I

RESPONSIBILITY TO PARENTS (OBEDIENCE)

"I want to make my child responsible!"

The phrase and the desire are common ones, but we usually think of it too generally. What does *responsible* mean? Well, it means *dependable*, it means *mature*, it means *reliable*, right?

In a way, yes. But it means more. *Responsibility* is a different kind of word from these apparent synonyms. *Responsible* needs a *to* behind it. Responsibility is always *to* someone. When someone is mature, he is not mature to someone, he is simply mature, or reliable, or dependable. But when he is responsible, he is responsible *to* someone, or *for* something.

This is what makes responsibility such an interesting and potentially valuable concept. It is surrounded. It is connected on both sides. It is hooked to someone and to something.

The clearer the *to* and the *for* are, the easier it is for children to understand and gain responsibility. When they know exactly what they are responsible for and precisely who they are responsible to, the fact of responsibility is established, and all that is left is follow-through.

The first subject childen can learn to be responsible to is you, their parent.

In that context, it is quite easy to decide what you would like them to be responsible for. They should be responsible to you first for obedience because they are your children. Second, they should become responsible for the things they have received. Third, they should gain responsibility for portions of the family work because they are part of your family.

These three responsibilities—obedience, things, and work—are closely tied together, not only because they are all responsibilities to you, but because they feed and grow on each other. Much of a child's obedience relates to caring for his things and doing his work. A child learns to take care of his things through the experience of work and of obedience. And a child learns to be responsible for work largely in response to obedience and in pursuit of things.

The responsibilities of things and work are particularly closely associated because children cannot feel fully responsible for things until they feel as though they own those things, and they rarely feel that they own them unless they have had to work for them.

Responsibility for Obedience
... from obeying parents to obeying laws

Obedience is the first step on the responsibility staircase. Without it, other forms of responsibility are hard to reach.

A. Definition and Illustration

Children who have learned to be responsible to earthly parents will find it natural to be responsible to a heavenly parent. This chapter frames and simplifies this most basic form of responsibility in order to give earthly parents some insights on how to "make it happen."

Lucy, a precocious five-year-old, had a particular quality that sometimes delighted her parents and sometimes infuriated them. When it was delighting them, they called it "individuality," "a strong will," "uniqueness." When it was infuriating them, they called it "stubbornness," "defiance," "cussedness."

In its second form, the quality included extreme and intense disobedience. When Lucy was told to come to dinner, she always had an excuse. When she was told to put away her toys, she dillied and dallied and never quite got it done. When she was told to turn off the TV and put on her pajamas, she often said, simply, "No."

To be sure, this irritated her parents, but Lucy's will was usually stronger than theirs. They had other things on their minds, and it was usually easier to drop the point than to force Lucy to mind. Occasionally, either because the disobedience became unbearably blatant or because other pressures had lowered the boiling point, father or mother would enforce a point, tell Lucy to either do it or else, and usually end up spanking her when she chose the "or else."

Recently, as often happens with four- and five-year-olds, Lucy's favorite word had become "why." She sometimes linked the word in a great chain of "whys" that tied her parents in knots. "*Why* do I have to eat those peas?" "*Why* will they make me grow big?" "*Why* does everyone have to get big?" "*Why* did Heavenly Father make it that way?"

Lucy's parents resorted to the answer that hog-tied parents have resorted to for generations: "Because I said so, that's why." Even that didn't stop Lucy. She said, "*Why* do you say so?" On another, particularly defiant day she said, "You'll have to come up with a better reason than that!"

One morning Lucy's mother heard a speaker discuss the topic "It should be easy to obey God." He made three points: (1) We must understand that God's laws are loving counsel from a wise Father, and keeping them minimizes hurt and maximizes happiness. (2) We must realize that God and His laws are absolutely consistent and that they will always apply, always be enforced. (3) We must comprehend that God does not want obedience to satisfy His ego needs. He wants obedience to His eternal, unchanging laws so that we can obtain their rewards and avoid their punishments.

That evening Lucy's parents had a long discussion about applying these principles to their own amateur parenthood. The three principles all seemed applicable, appropriate, and needed. Could they, with Lucy's assistance, develop some clear and simple family laws? Could Lucy be helped to understand the reasons for each law and to think in terms of obeying laws rather than obeying people? Could they apply the laws, along with their rewards and punishments, clearly and consistently? Could Lucy learn that the laws were a manifestation of her parents' love for her and that keeping the laws brought happiness?

Yes to each question! They took the time to hold family councils to explain to Lucy the general and the specific concepts involved, to let her put in her ideas and to vote on theirs.

Almost instantly, obedience took on a different meaning in the home—and in Lucy's mind. Instead of a contest of the will where the bigger people could win by force, obedience became simply a question of whether one wanted the positive or negative consequences, the rewards or the penalties. The same precociousness and strong will that had previously made Lucy so unmanageable now made her intrigued with the new concept of laws and determined to live them and prove them.

Under the new system, Lucy's life (not to mention that of her parents) became happier and simpler. The family laws were readjusted occasionally, always in conference with Lucy, to fit new circumstances.

There was, however, one remaining obedience problem in Lucy's home. Lucy had learned to respect and obey *laws*, but still had problems obeying *parents* in nonlaw situations. She did well on things like "get ready for bed now," because bedtime was a family law. She could tell time, and it was the clock that decided when she should go to bed, not her parents. But problems still existed with things, such as, "Lucy, you better wear your coat today, it's a little chilly," or "Turn the TV off now, you've watched enough for one day." That sort of command was, to Lucy, a judgment call, and she was still very much in possession of her strong will. She even managed to turn the new family law structure to her side of the argument by saying, "Well, there's no law about *that*!"

Some areas of difficulty were overcome easily by creating a new family law. The family did, for example, agree on a policy regulating the amount of television to be seen each week, but to list too many laws diluted their importance, and there were always situations that would not fall under the jurisdiction of even a very long list.

The problem was solved (or at least a big step taken toward its solution) one evening when Lucy's father was in a particularly good mood because of a business deal. He asked Lucy to pick up some papers that the dog had pulled out of the wastebasket. Lucy gave him the "There's-no-law-about-that" routine. Instead of taking his usual "I-don't-care-if-there's-a-law-or-not-you-mind-your-father" stance, he sat down, cross-legged, on the floor with Lucy and did some explaining:

"Lucy, let me tell you a story, a true one. Parts of it you've already heard. Long ago, before we came to live on this world, we lived in heaven with our Heavenly Father. He made this world for us so we could come down and have families of our own and learn to love each other and learn to follow his laws. He worked it out so that some of us would come down first and grow up so we could be the mommies and daddies for some of the others. You'll grow up and be a mommy for some who are still up there now.

"Heavenly Father knew that when he sent us down as babies, we would need parents to help us learn how to be good. He wants parents to be responsible for their children. That means to teach them and care for them and love them until they are old enough to be on their own. When children don't learn to be obedient, Heavenly Father says it's the parents' fault. When mommy and I asked him to send us a little baby, we promised him we would be responsible for you and take care of you. If we didn't love you, we might let you do anything you wanted, and not have any laws and not tell you the right things to do.

"Good mommies and daddies have the responsibility to know what's best for their children and be sure they do it. And good children have the responsibility to obey their parents.

"I promise you that Mommy and I will try our hardest to make only good laws and to ask you to do only things we think are best. That is our responsibility. And your responsibility is to obey us. That way you'll learn obedience and be able to obey Heavenly Father's laws too.

"Now, I think you should pick up those papers. Everyone in our family needs to help around the house, and I asked you to do that because it's good for you to help."

As time passed, Lucy's parents came to feel that there were two basic keys to Lucy's obedience. One key was to have a basic set of well-understood, family laws so that in most situations she was obeying a law rather than a person. The second key was to have a clear understanding of parent responsibility and child obedience-responsibility to cover behavior that did not fall under one of the family laws.

In our own family, particularly with our first children,

obedience never seemed quite obtainable. We worked hard at it, with methods ranging from militaristic "yes-sir" type obedience to more subtle efforts involving code words designed to remind children to do something without coming right out and telling them.

What follows are some of the methods that work, not just in the mechanical sense of "getting children to obey," but in the deeper sense of helping them understand *why* they should obey and in building a foundation of parental obedience on which to build the superstructure of responsibility in their lives.

B. Methods

1. *Story: "Cheekey and the Laws."* (This story, taken from the book *Teaching Children Joy* is a good place to begin for small children.)

Cheekey was a baby monkey. He lived with his sister and his mother and father in a tree. Their tree was in the jungle. In the jungle there were some laws. They were called Jungle Laws. Do you know what laws are? (Things that you must do right or else you get punishment.)

Do you know what a punishment is? (Something sad that happens when you break a law.)

There were two laws in Cheekey's jungle. One was that whenever you were in a tree, you had to hold on with your hand, or your foot, or your tail. What do you think the punishment was if you broke that law? (You would fall!)

The other jungle law was that if you saw a lion coming, you had to quickly climb up a tree. What do you think the punishment was if you broke that law? (You would get eaten up!)

In Cheekey's own family tree, there were two family laws. One law was that you couldn't go out of the tree without asking. Why do you think they had that law? (So Cheekey wouldn't get lost.)

Why didn't his mother and father want him to get lost? (Because they loved him.)

What do you think the punishment was if Cheekey went out of his tree without asking? (His mother gave him a little swat with her tail right on his bottom.)

Why did his mother do that? (So he wouldn't go out of the tree again.)

Why didn't she want him to do it again? (Because she loved him and didn't want him to get lost.)

The other monkey family law was to never drop your banana peels on limbs of the family tree. Why do you think they had that law? (So no one would slip on them and fall out of the tree.)

Why did the monkey family decide to have a law like that? (Because they loved each other and didn't want anyone in their family to get hurt.)

What do you think the punishment was for breaking that law? (A little swat on the bottom.)

Why would the mother do that? (Because she loved Cheekey and wanted him to remember not to do it again.)

Now, I'm going to tell you the things that happened to Cheekey one day. Sometimes there were laws to tell him what to do and sometimes there weren't any laws and he could decide for himself.

When Cheekey first woke up in the morning, he had to stretch and yawn, and he almost let go of the branch. Was there a law to tell him what to do? (Yes—hold on or he would fall.)

Then he looked at his two hats, a red one and a green one. Was there a law to tell him which one to wear? (No—he could choose whichever one he wanted. He chose the red one.)

Then he wanted to climb down out of the tree to find a banana for breakfast. Was there a law to tell him what to do? (Yes—ask his mother so she would know where he was and so he wouldn't get lost.)

He found a big banana and a little banana. Was there a law to tell him which one to choose? (No—he could choose either one he wished.) Cheekey chose the big one because he was very hungry.

While he was walking back to his tree, he saw a lion. Was there a law to tell him what to do? (Yes— climb up a tree quickly or the lion would eat him!)

Cheekey climbed up a tree. After the lion went away he went back to his own tree and wondered which limb to sit on to eat the banana. Was there a law to tell him where to sit? (No—he could choose any limb he wanted.)

When he peeled the banana, was there a law about the peel? (Yes—don't leave it on a limb.)

Cheekey had a fun, safe day. It's fun and safe when you know the laws and do what they say and it's fun to decide things when there isn't a law about them.

2. *Comparison story: The Smiths and the Joneses.* (To help small children want to have family laws and want to live them.)

Draw (or let the children draw) on a blackboard or large sheet of paper two houses, similar in size, next door to each other. Using it as a visual aid, tell the following story in your own words:

"In this house (*point to one of the houses*) lived the Smith family. They had a boy and a girl named Steve and Sue. And they had *no* family laws. They didn't have to come to dinner at any certain time or go to bed at any certain time. They didn't have to put away their toys; they didn't have to mind their mother and father; they could watch TV anytime they wanted. In fact, their parents let them do just about anything they wanted. (*Point to the other house.*) In this house lived the Jones family. They had a boy named Jimmy and a girl named Janie. They had family laws, and the children knew that they would be punished if they broke the laws.

"Now let's pretend we can see right inside each of these houses and watch what is happening. Let's look into the Smith house first. Look at Steve and Sue's rooms. They look like pigpens. Nothing is put away; everything is on the floor. But where are Steve and Sue? Oh, there's Sue watching TV. Her homework's not done. She'll be sorry tomorrow when her teacher asks her a question and she doesn't know the answer. There's Steve across the fence playing with a friend. His mom called him for dinner, but he didn't come. Now his food is cold and soggy. Look, his face is scratched from a fight with Sue over a toy. They don't even have laws against fighting.

"Let's look inside the Jones house. Jimmy's and Janie's clothes and toys are all neat and tidy, because their family has a law about that. Their family members are all sitting together having a nice dinner, because they have a law about that. Jimmy and Janie did their homework before dinner, because they have a law for that. When they've finished eating, they will be able to play and not worry about school tomorrow."

Make your story personal by including things that are relevant to your family. Then involve the children in a discussion based on the following questions: Are laws good or bad? Do they make us happy or sad? Would we like to be like the Smiths? Should grown-ups have to obey laws too? What are some of our national laws? What are some of our community laws? What are some of our church laws? What are some of our family laws? How does each make us happy?

3. *Role playing.* (To help children realize that parents are responsible to God for them and that the children's responsibility is to obey.)

Let a couch or table represent our premortal life. Have an older child be Heavenly Father listening to the prayer of the parents who are "down" on earth. Have other children be "up there" with Heavenly Father.

The parents pray for a baby and tell Heavenly Father that they will take care of him, teach him to do right, and be responsible for him until he is old enough to know things for himself.

Then Heavenly Father selects one of the children to "go

down." He instructs him to listen to his parents and obey them so that he can one day be a parent himself. He tells the child that he will start as a baby and that it will take many years to grow up. His parents will help him and will know what is best for him. He should obey their laws just as he obeys God's laws. If he does obey their laws, he will grow up to be a good parent himself and will someday return to be with Heavenly Father. He will be tempted by Satan, who wants him not to obey his parents, but he should remember that obedience will make him happy, and disobedience will not.

Then the child "goes down" and pretends to be a baby. The parents hold him, love him, and tell him they will do all they can to teach him to do right.

4. *Family council.* (To formalize family laws that children help create and thus feel responsible for keeping.)

Sit down together with a blank chart and marking pens and hold a family council to create (or formalize) your family laws.

Indicate that anyone can propose a law, but that it won't be put on the chart until it is discussed and voted for unanimously by the family.

Steer the discussion in such a way that the laws are simple and direct. Don't end up with too many. Arrive together at an appropriate "punishment" for the breaking of each law. Use "natural consequences" or a close approximation of them for punishments wherever possible. For example, the punishment for not coming on time to dinner could be no dinner. The punishment for not cleaning one's room could be staying in the room until it is clean. The punishment for yelling or screaming could be going in one's room where others don't have to listen. If spanking is to be a punishment, it should be used for serious violations that hurt others.

Write the agreed-on punishment beside the law to which it applies. Vote on the punishment as well as the laws. Discuss each until everyone is in agreement.

Keep the laws visible. Enforce them consistently. Alter them as needed, but only through further family councils.

5. *Family council to make mutual commitments.* (To make parent directives more thoughtful and child obedience more predictable.)

Gather the family together and tell the children that you want them to know of some commitments that you (as parents) have made. Explain that you not only love each of the children more than anything else, but that you feel that they are your greatest responsibility and the most important thing Heavenly Father has given you.

Tell them that you want to make them a very special promise and to ask them to make a promise to you in return.

Your promise is that you will do your very best to be wise parents, to help them to be wise, and to always say and do the things that you feel are best for them. Promise them that you will pray for God's help in knowing what is best for them. Tell them that you won't give them everything they want or let them do everything they want, because that would not be wise, and because you love them too much to give up your responsibility for them.

As you make these serious promises, look each one in the eye, and speak to him on his own level.

Then ask them for a promise in return—a promise of obedience, a promise that they will obey you and obey the family laws. Ask that their promise be as serious and sincere as yours.

Do anything you can to make the moment memorable and the promises lasting. You may wish to conclude by raising your hands together and making a "joint pledge."

6. *Role reversal.* (To help children see things from your perspective, and you from theirs.)

When a serious disagreement arises concerning obedience in a particular matter, sit back for a moment, let things calm down, and then ask the child to pretend he's the mommy or daddy and you are the child. Set the stage for him. Tell him *why* he wants his child to do (or not do) the particular thing. Then start the game.

Be a convincing "child." Play his role well and make him explain to you why he wants you to obey.

Some children role-play more naturally than others, but all children can learn the technique, and often it can be very helpful.

C. Family Focal Points: Family Laws and "Trigger Words"

Many years ago, when our oldest daughters were four and three, we created our first "Family Law Chart." I had written the story "Cheekey and the Laws" to help them understand the concept. We had talked of laws as things that make a home orderly and happy. Now we sat down to let the children help us formulate our set of laws. We told them that laws were to tell us the things we must do and the things we must not do.

Lo and behold, they understood! Saren's hand went up and our first law was proposed: "Don't ruin things that aren't for ruining!" We all voted yes on that one. She had another one: "Don't hit little other girls." Another unanimous vote. Then Shawnie got into the act. She remembered a scolding she had received earlier that day for playing with an electrical plug and outlet. "Don't pud in puds." We went on until we had sixteen laws—too many, but certainly better than none.

We still have that original law chart, but it has been replaced by several new editions.

A few years later we discussed and listed punishments—a specific one for each law. Still later, Saren approached me one night and said, "Dad, our laws are too complicated and there are too many of them. The little kids can't even remember them all." That led to a simplification process. If the Lord could make do with ten commandments, we ought to be able to handle our little family with five.

We ended up with five one-word laws:
1. Peace
2. Order
3. Asking
4. Obedience
5. "Pegs"

"Peace" includes things ranging from the original "Don't hit little other girls" to loud words, anger, or screaming. "Order" covers leaving rooms in order, taking out only one toy at a time, and putting away anything you use. "Asking" means never going somewhere, or using something of someone else's, without asking. "Obedience" means minding mother and father (more on that in a moment). And "Pegs" means getting the pegs (which represent family jobs and procedures) in our family peg-board each day (discussed in detail in chapter 6).

Punishments for violation of each law are clearly defined and appear on the law chart.

Much of the disobedience that occurs in families is often simply a bad habit. Children give excuses, whine, say "That's not fair," largely out of a pattern that they get into. We made some progress in breaking that habit through a very simple process of "trigger words."

We held a family council (much like the one discussed in method 5 in this chapter) where we pledged our care and best efforts to the children and they pledged obedience to us. Then we decided that we needed a signal to give to the children that meant, "We've thought about what we're asking you to do. We think it is best, and you should obey." Then they, in turn, needed a simple signal or trigger word that would indicate to us that they understood. They needed a "habit-word" that prompted the good habit of obedience.

We picked the simplest words: *please* from us, and *Yes, Mommy* or *Yes, Daddy* from them. If I say, "Josh, time to put that away and get ready for bed" and he starts to say, "Oh, but Daddy can't I just—," I say, "Please," which is his trigger to say, "Yes, Daddy," and do it.

The word *please* needs to be used carefully. Sometimes it may be well to let Josh do "just one more thing." But the point is, when the parent says "please" (or whatever other trigger-word is decided on), the child knows it is a clear request and is obligated to say "Yes, Daddy" and do it instantly.

In our family, the law chart is the ongoing focal point for law-obedience, and the trigger words are the focal point for parent-obedience. Together they can help even very small children learn this first aspect of responsibility.

Remember that laws and obedience are not only the first rung of the responsibility ladder, but they are also tremendous sources of security to children. A home that is ordered and based on clear procedures and rules of conduct, a home where authority is clearly defined, a home with consistency and discipline—such a home is the most secure and confidence-breeding environment in which a child's life can take shape.

Please don't assume, after you sit down as a family and carefully draw up the family laws and punishments, that somehow your children will turn into lovely, obedient angels overnight. The principles involved are true, and they work, but not without much ado. We have had at least twenty-five family home evenings in which we have discussed family laws. After every violation, we talk about them. We have defended our purpose in using them and enforcing them. The children have talked about them with each other, and we have somehow managed to drag them with us through the complaints and hard times. Obedience in children does not develop overnight, especially when the children are not used to the idea of following laws or to being obedient. It is just not easy!

It is a valuable exercise to sit down as parents and think about the obedience level in your own family. It is easy to get so used to certain responses from our children that we don't even realize that they're not being obedient.

I recall an experience several years ago when we had just

arrived in England. Joyce, an outspoken young English girl who was helping me one day, couldn't help hearing a conversation between me and our oldest daughter, Saren (who was six). It was quite a heated conversation. After it was over and Saren disappeared, Joyce said to me, "Why do you let Saren talk to you like that?"

"Like what?" I asked, amazed that she would think it was peculiar.

"Like she did this afternoon when you were 'having words' with her. Americans seem to let their children speak to them in such a dreadful manner!"

I was shocked, but I've come to be grateful to Joyce for that question, because it might otherwise have taken me quite some time to recognize that Saren really did have a nasty tone in her voice when she disagreed with me. She had been speaking with near contempt. I simply had tuned out the offensiveness in her voice because I'd heard it often. But in thinking about it, I decided that Joyce was absolutely right and that things were going to change!

"It's all right to ask questions," I told Saren that evening, "but you must remember to use a respectful tone of voice."

Occasionally she ventures too near the line, but when I give her a certain signal, she remembers and calms down.

The same principle applies to obedience. We parents get so used to giving orders that we don't really expect to be carried out that the children's ears become deaf and our minds become numb to the facts. Children will do exactly what their parents expect. They are very perceptive, and they do know exactly what is expected of them. A soul-searching family conference on the subject is highly recommended. It may change lots of bad habits that you hardly realized were there.

It is also important to remember that even though children know they should be obedient and are trying, some try harder than others. We have one particular child who occasionally has a more difficult time than the others in being obedient. I realize even as I write that instructions have been *going in one ear and out the other for several days. She has to be asked to do her jobs several times and still may not finish them. It's time for a private consultation with this child to review the laws, talk about minding, and recommit her to the principle of her obedience. A one-on-one relationship often helps to correct things, but it still takes consistent follow-through and special emphasis until she feels good about her obedience again.*

The point is that teaching obedience is not easy and does not involve one or two easy lessons. So don't be discouraged. Persevere! It will make you happy, and most important, it will make your children happy. In spite of all they say, they love to obey!

Responsibility for Things...
from pajamas to money 5

It is unlikely that a child will accept responsibilities that he cannot see, such as gifts, potential, jobs, or character, until he accepts responsibilities he can see—his things.

A. Definition and Illustration

Most of us have too many material possessions. As our society becomes more complex and our lives have more and more facets, "things" can begin to overtake us. More than ever before it is necessary, in order to live happily in this world, to simplify, organize, and be responsible for things. The goal of this chapter is to offer some precise suggestions to parents about how to get children to feel and accept this responsibility and to learn to control things before things control them!

George and Nancy Cuthbert were meticulous people. Some would have called them perfectionists. Everything had a place, and everything was in that place. Disorderliness drove them crazy. Perhaps the fact that they were both that way is what attracted them to each other in the first place.

They had been married for nearly ten years and had three children. Their oldest child, Jimmy, was proof of the heredity factor. He was as neat and tidy as they were. His room looked as though it were ready to be photographed for a better-homemaking article.

But the next two children, Ginny, eight, and Phillip, six, were another story. No amount of coaxing, bribing, punishing, or encouraging could persuade them to take care of their things. Their rooms looked as if they had been hit by a hurricane. Though Nancy cleaned their rooms often, five minutes later they once again looked as if a hurricane had struck.

Finally, Nancy had had it. She decided that if they wanted to live in filth and disarray, it was just too bad. She decided to never look in their rooms at all. When she found one of their toys or an article of clothing scattered elsewhere in the house (a frequent occurrence), she marched to the door of the offender's room, turned her head the other way, opened the door, threw the article in, then quickly slammed the door shut again.

Ginny and Phillip didn't seem to notice. The only perceptible changes in them were that they looked a little more rumpled each day, and they asked Nancy more often where things were.

"In your room," she always said.

"But *where* in our room?" they always said.

"I don't know. I haven't been in there for days," she always said.

"Why not?" they always asked.

"Because I don't like to go in messy places," she always said. Then they usually walked away, looking a bit confused.

It wasn't a technique. Nancy had given up on all the techniques. This was just her way of giving up altogether on the whole idea of making them responsible.

One day Ginny came into the kitchen and said, "Mom, where is that red blouse I like?"

Nancy said, "In your room," and the conversation followed its standard pattern.

Finally, Ginny said, "Well, it's gone, so you'll have to buy me another one."

"Not so," said Nancy. "When you own a thing and lose it, it's gone."

"Well, it's not really mine," said Ginny. "You bought it."

Nancy thought about that for a while. That afternoon she went to visit her sister's family. They had just returned from a year-long assignment in another city and had returned to their house only to discover how poorly the renters had cared for it. "People just don't take care of things unless they own them," her sister said.

Nancy made the connection in her mind. Ginny and Phillip somehow didn't perceive of their things as *theirs*. They hadn't worked for them, and therefore they didn't value them.

But ownership wasn't the only reason for neatness, orderliness, and care, was it? After all, Jimmy had always taken care of his things, even when he was small, just for the pleasure and convenience of having things where they belonged.

During the next few days, while Nancy and George were trying to think of a way to help Ginny and Phillip feel the responsibility of ownership, their constantly messy rooms began to have an effect. Nancy had taken a couple of peeks in, and the levels of rubbish were now nearly knee-deep. She also noticed one day that Phillip had tried to pick up a few things to make a path in his room.

Then came an unexpected breakthrough. Ginny came downstairs one day and said, "Mom, will you help me clean up my room, please?"

"Whatever for?" said Nancy.

"I'm just getting sick of it like that," said Ginny, "and besides, I can't find anything."

Nancy acted on her first impulse. "Does Phillip feel the same way?"

"I think so," replied Ginny.

"Then get him down here, and let's make a deal."

When they were both sitting in front of her, Nancy said, "Okay, here's the deal. I'll help each of you clean your room this one time, but they are *your* rooms, and from now on it's *your* responsibility to keep your things put away. From now on, whenever I see anything left out or in the wrong place, I won't put it away, and I won't throw it on the floor of your room either. What I will do is put it on your bed. Then every night before bedtime you have to take the things off your bed and put them away. Is it a deal?"

The children agreed. There were some regressions now and then, but basically the plan worked. They soon found that a bed full of toys and clothes was a very unpleasant thing to confront at night when they were tired, so they gradually left less and less out of place.

Nancy and George realized that not all children are the

same. Some, like Jimmy, are motivated to take care of things out of their simple attraction to neatness. Others take care of things only when there are practical, *ownership* reasons for doing so. They eventually found a way to give their children a stronger sense of ownership to supplement the "things-on-the-bed" method. They developed a system of paying Ginny and Phillip for some general household jobs they did and arranging other ways of helping them earn their own money which they used to buy their own toys and clothes. Over time, this approach worked even better than the "things-on-the-bed," because it provided an actual fact of worked-for ownership. Where the "bed" method had been merely a technique, the ownership method was more of a principle; it worked on the basis of pride and of genuine care for one's own things. (This "ownership" method is explained in more detail in the "family focal point" of this chapter.)

The more we analyze teaching the responsibility for material things, the more we realize, once again, that the key to success is remembering the never-ending quest to improve ourselves.

I have a confession to make. I am not a Nancy or a George. I am not a naturally tidy person. I somehow managed to blunder through high school and college excusing my disastrous room with obligations to practice and leadership responsibilities at school. My dad used to jokingly call me "Mrs. Smith," the name of a particularly disorganized neighbor. (One day I asked to use her phone, and after picking my way through the debris to the phone, I turned around to see their dead Christmas tree still decorated in the corner. It was March.)

At college I was "blessed" with a roommate who was exactly like me, and though we both did well in school and were gone most of the time studying or practicing, we always returned to a room that looked very much as though someone had thrown a hand grenade in and shut the door. Occasionally I'd turn over a new leaf, but it was short-lived.

It seems to me that I improved for a while after our marriage, thinking how embarrassed I'd be if he found out how bad I was. As children came along, however, things began to get muddled again, and I began getting up in the morning to a sink full of dirty dishes that I was just too tired to wash the night before.

After four children and many, many commitments to try harder, I finally reached the point where I could no longer tolerate the messy rooms at night, the lost shoes, clothes, scissors, papers, and so forth. We decided in earnest that the time had arrived. All the "wouldn't it be nice" ideas were to be implemented. I quickly realized that any plan had to start with me, the mother!

A good friend taught me the principle of touching things only once, which helped immensely. For example, if your recipe calls for salt, take it from the cupboard, put it in the mix, and return it to the cupboard all in one movement. When washing clothes, put the item straight from the dryer into a basket labeled for the appropriate person. The list goes on and on, but as I implemented the principle, I found that the clutter began to disappear.

All in all, I can honestly say that since I have started putting away all my own things, seeing that my own bed was the first one made, and have followed through with the children's responsibility for their things, our home has been a different place. I would not have believed that it could make so much difference!

Our favorite scripture is Doctrine and Covenants 88:119, which states: "Organize yourselves; prepare every needful thing; and establish a house, even a house of prayer, a house of fasting, a house of faith, a house of learning, a house of glory, a house of order, a house of God." (Emphasis added.) We believe that if we do the organizing and establish the order, then all that is in between will follow.

Again, it is not easy! This has been one of the hardest aspects of parenting for me, maybe because I was so bad at it. But I testify that the reward is certainly worth the effort.

B. Methods

1. Family laws. (To help children see that orderliness and care of one's things is an expected and mandatory part of membership in the family.)

As discussed in chapter 1, simple, clear, high-awareness-level family laws are the most basic way to establish behavior patterns. One law should deal with the care and orderliness of each person's things. The punishment connected with violation of this law should tie directly to the problem itself. A child should have to stay in his room until it's clean—he eats no dinner until it is. Or, if the "things-on-the-bed" method is used, he should have to put each thing in its place before his bedtime. The idea is to show the very real inconvenience and unpleasantness of not caring for one's things.

As with all family laws, the keys to effectiveness are simple but not easy. They are: First, be sure the law is understood. Children must participate in and vote on its creation and must know exactly what is required and precisely what the punishment is for breaking it. Second, be consistent. Laws that are enforced erratically not only do little or no good, they actually can do harm by teaching children that laws are made to be broken.

2. Example. (To show children that being responsible for one's things is a source of satisfaction and joy, and to be sure that they know how to care for their things.)

Bring your children in to watch as you put away your own things, as you shine your shoes, as you put away your tools or kitchen utensils. Let them see that you have a place for each thing. Let them watch you wash the car or oil the lawnmower or polish the silver. Let them see the pride you feel in caring for your things. Don't lecture them or make the connections to them too obvious. Instead of saying, "See how well I take care of my things? You should take good care of your things too," say, "I really like to take care of my things; it makes me feel happy inside" or "It's fun to have a place for everything and put everything in its right place. I feel good when everything is neat and clean."

3. *Ownership tags.* (To help smaller children realize that certain things are theirs, and that they are responsible for them.)

Little round self-stick tags with the child's name on them can go a long way toward helping each child to put toys and other belongings away. Particularly in the early years, when children have just learned to write their names, those names are a source of pride and identity to them. Seeing their names on articles not only helps to establish the ideas of ownership and responsibility; it also creates a desire to "care for" and to "take pride in."

4. *"In-place" tags or outlines.* (To help children connect a certain thing with a certain place.)

We've all seen the mechanic's workroom or the woodworker's tool wall on which the shadow outline of a tool or wrench is painted on the surface where the tool hangs or the shelf where it sits. A similar system can help children get it into their minds that their own things each have a particular place.

A variation of this idea also works with clothes. One drawer can be labeled *socks* (either with a picture or the word), a certain shelf labeled *shoes*, and so forth.

5. *Simplification.* (To make the whole concept of responsibility for things simpler by simply having fewer things.)

While it may not be a method, this is perhaps the most effective of all ways to teach children to be responsible for their things. In so many families there are simply too many things. Children have too many toys, too many clothes, too much to keep track of.

We learned this lession graphically when we began spending our summers at a small lakeside cabin in Idaho. Because the cabin is small, the children are allowed to bring only a couple of toys each. Because it is a lake and because it is summer, they take only a swimming suit, one set of church clothes, and two sets of play clothes. It is heavenly! Nothing is out of place, because there are so few things!

The key in everyday situations is to simplify and to aim for quality rather than for quantity. Give a child one long-lasting, high-quality Christmas present that he will care for and treasure rather than a dozen cheap things with planned obsolescence that, at worst, break or tear or become unusable in a week, and at best, hold his interest only briefly and then become part of the clutter.

The starting point is to clear everything out, get rid of all the low-quality, high-quantity junk—and of some nice things too, if they are not often used and if they are poorly cared for. Give them to the needy, to someone who will value them.

One effective way to rid yourself of superfluous things is the "gunny-bag" method discussed in the "family focal point" section of this chapter.

6. *"Pride" sign.* (To help children discover a feeling of pride in their own neatness and care of their things.)

One rainy Saturday I took three of our children (the messiest three, ages four, six, and eight) into my den and let them watch me clean it. I tried to express the satisfaction I felt from having things in place and cared for. They were moderately interested.

When I finished, I taped a large, brightly colored sign on the den door that said PRIDE. I didn't say anything about it, but, of course, they asked.

"*Pride* means that I'm proud of how my den looks," I said. "It means that I feel good because all my things are clean and neat."

"Can I get one of those on my door?" the six-year-old, predictably, asked first, and the other two chimed in.

"Yes, but first your rooms will have to be as neat as my den."

It worked. It still works. The signs go up periodically, whenever we need a booster on basic neatness.

It's not the sign that is important; it's the discussion and reinforcement built around it. Talk about how good neatness feels. Talk about how lucky we are to have certain things; talk about how much some people would like to have those things, and how well they would take care of them if they did have them.

7. *Their goal.* (To help children feel that their effort to take responsibility for things is their idea as well as yours, and that it pleases them as well as you when they do well.)

One of the key methods referred to repeatedly in this book is the Sunday goal-setting sessions (described in detail in chapter 12).

Once you feel that a child has a basic grasp of the benefits of caring for his things, encourage him to make it one of his weekly goals to deal with it. A small child might have the goal of making his bed each day for a week without being asked or reminded. An older child might have a goal of reorganizing his room and establishing an exact place for everything.

When it is their objective, children will move toward real assumption of responsibility for things. Until it becomes their goal, they are not really accepting responsibility.

C. Family Focal Points: "Gunny Bag," "Bed Throw," and "Own Money"

One day several years ago, I came home to find a terrific mess in the downstairs playroom and children's bedrooms. It was one of those particularly irritating messes of clutter—small, cheap toys, and various bits and pieces that no one really claimed as theirs, but that seemed to get kicked around the house constantly.

I took a deep breath, ready to call for the children to "get down here and straighten up this pig pen," but before the words came out, I had a different idea. After all, I'd yelled those words before, and there had certainly been no lasting effect.

Instead, I found a large old cloth laundry bag and painted on it two large "monster eyes" and a nose, positioned so that the bag's draw-string opening was a mouth. Then I started making monster noises and dragging the bag around the house, putting any scattered or out-of-place articles into it.

It took only a couple of minutes to attract a full child audience, more amused than worried at this point, shouting, "What are you doing?" and "Who is that?"

"This is Gunny Bag," I said. "He lives in the attic, and every once in a while, without warning, he comes down here and gobbles up all the toys or clothes that are left lying around out of place." I tried to sound matter-of-fact and went right on "eating" the toys.

The children watched at first, then started asking questions like, "Can we get the things back?"

The answer was "Yes, on Saturday he spits them all up in a big pile, and if they are put right away, he doesn't eat them again. If they are left out, though, he gobbles them right up, and once he has eaten anything for the second time, he never spits it up again!"

Their eyes were wider now, and there was an occasional "Oh no, not that, Daddy." "It's not me eating them," I reminded them. "It's Gunny Bag."

In a few more moments they gave up talking and began scurrying about, trying to rescue their best things. But the Gunny Bag "ate" quite a lot, and the children got the message.

Since then, Gunny Bag has returned often. He is always unannounced, always a surprise. When he finds nothing out of place "to eat" in a given room, he cries miserably, much to the delight of the child who has thwarted him through his neatness.

Over time, Gunny Bag has accomplished two very worthwhile things for our family. First, he engenders the need to always keep things neat and tidy, since no one ever knows when he will descend from his lair in the attic. Second, he is like a good garden snake who eats up all the destructive insects. He gobbles up the little, unnecessary toys and objects that clutter a house, and once he has eaten something twice, it never comes back (it goes, in fact, to the welfare store). Thus Gunny Bag weeds out the unnecessary things and causes the necessary and valuable things to be kept securely in their places.

In addition to Gunny Bag, we like to use the "things-on-the-bed" method that Nancy and George discovered at the beginning of this chapter. Children visually see the things they've left out accumulating in one concentrated spot on their beds and thus become more conscious of those things and more aware of the inconvenience they cause their parents and themselves by leaving them out.

A key thing that children must sooner or later learn responsibility for is money. We have decided that sooner is much better than later because accepting responsibility for money is the key to being responsible about other things.

About the time our oldest daughter turned eight, we realized that we were not comfortable with the money situation between us and her. An allowance seemed so normal, yet I felt we were teaching the wrong principle by giving something for nothing. I had had many friends whose parents had given them money all their lives. Some were able to handle that until they were old enough to find a better substitute. Others seemed to rely on the dole forever. I saw roommates in college whose lives were controlled by how much their fathers sent in a particular month. Others were totally irresponsible with the money they were given, probably indicative of the attitude "It isn't mine anyway."

During the same time period, I was having trouble getting our two oldest girls to pick up their clothes and to practice their music without nagging and artificial rewards. I had tried everything from self-stick stars on charts to lollipops. Suddenly one day I thought of a solution—the same method my mother had used with me. Why hadn't I thought of it before?

Recognizing that it is hard (though not impossible) for an eight-year-old to earn money in the outside world, we decided to kill two birds with one stone and pay her for practicing. Now before you label that "absurd bribery," let us explain.

We began by offering a small amount for each half hour of practice. Two half-hour sessions were expected each day, one on violin and one on piano. Next we proclaimed that if all the practicing had been completed at the end of the week (one hour each day), our daughter's money would be doubled. We calculated it so that it would take a month or so to save enough for a dress or a pair of shoes. In some cases we allowed an IOU to be written if just the right dress was found but funds were not yet earned.

It worked like a dream. As if by magic, her lovely new clothes were hung in the closet instead of left on the floor, because now they were really hers. Since then, we have had no trouble getting our oldest daughter to practice.

The second child has followed suit. She also earns money by practicing, but in her case there is even more interest in making money by babysitting for me. By the time she was nine she was probably one of the world's best babysitters. We paid her very low wages to start with, knowing that her need for money would increase with age, and so that she could feel that her raises are due to experience and excellent work.

By the time our oldest son was seven, he was a real entrepreneur. Although he is not as interested in clothes as the girls, he's fascinated with calculators and chemistry sets. He is not practicing music on a regular basis yet, but he is very much interested in Saturday jobs! (We also pay the children for individual Saturday jobs not included in their regular responsibilities.) On Saturday mornings he hounds us about what he can do to earn some money for something he's seen at the store. Next summer he also plans to raise potatoes (as he has the past two years), but next year, instead of giving them all to his family, he's planning to sell them door-to-door or from a stand on the corner.

Our children know they are on their own financially at age eight. (We make exceptions of special things on birthdays and Christmas, and for underclothes and socks, items they are less inclined to buy for themselves.)

Many creative ideas are generated when children want to earn their own money. Some children have natural good sense about money, and others have to learn by experience. Our premise, however, is that the time for children to learn these valuable lessons about money is when they are from eight to twelve years old. These lessons will greatly influence their happiness and freedom later in life.

Conclusion

During ages eight to twelve while the children do earn their own money and buy their own things, it is usually us that they earn it from. When they turn twelve, however, they are expected to earn it elsewhere—from paper routes, babysitting, and other out-of-the-home sources.

It is not only the earning of money but the handling of money that constitutes the beginning of fiscal responsibility. We have a "family bank" consisting of a large wooden chest with a combination lock on it. Each child (even the smaller ones who don't yet have "financial responsibility" but who do earn money for small jobs and errands) has a bank book in which deposits and withdrawals are recorded. The family bank pays exorbitant interest (10 percent every quarter—10 percent because the children can compute it easily). Children get a small "treat" out of the chest each time they make a deposit. The combined incentives of interest and a treat have made real savers out of our children—that and the fact that they quickly discover how soon their money is spent and gone if they don't put it into the bank.

Responsibility for Work...
from family jobs to family pride
6

"All work and no play" may make Jack a dull boy, but it doesn't happen very often today. The more frequent occurrence is *"all play and no work"*—and that makes Jack an irresponsible boy!

A. Definition and Illustration

Much of the satisfaction and joy of life comes from the acceptance and conscientious completion of work. Children who never learn to work not only fail to accomplish worthwhile things as adults, but they also forfeit one of the basic joys and fulfillments of life. In this chapter, we will explore ways that the responsibility of work can be simplified and given to children. We will also look at ways that the family work load can be shared so that it can be drudgery to none and joy to all.

Craig and SueAnn Peterson woke up late. It was Saturday morning. From the family room they heard the pops and bangs and laughter of the television cartoons. It was a pleasant way to wake up—pleasant except for what they had to face next: getting the children to do their weekly jobs.

They both felt that it was necessary and important for their three children to feel part of the responsibility for the house, for doing their share, for learning the basics of how to work.

It surely was unpleasant, though. SueAnn thought about it while lying in bed. First, the children would argue about who got the easiest job. Then they would dillydally around, get distracted, lose the broom, and generally do everything in their power to wiggle out of, or postpone, or half-finish the jobs.

Ten-year-old Allison, who should be setting the example, was the worst of all. The other two heard her complaining and followed suit. Allison was a very bright, very independent, and very stubborn child, and she was capable of marshaling a long list of fairly credible sounding reasons why she didn't want to, or couldn't, or shouldn't do her jobs.

"Actually, Mom, those are *your* jobs. Dad goes to work, we go to school, and you take care of the house. You don't have to go to work for dad or go to school for me, so why should I have to clean the house for you?"

SueAnn literally bit her tongue—to keep from biting Allison. She realized that there was a message in what Allison was saying, a message *about Allison*. Her daughter did not fully understand the shared responsibility of a family. She saw the jobs as arbitrary assignments from the only person she viewed as responsible for those jobs.

That night the Petersons had a serious family council. The conclusions reached during the meeting were simple and direct. Even Justin, their six-year-old, understood them.

1. We are all responsible for the house because we all live here and are part of a family.

2. Mom takes the biggest share of the burden because of dad's job and the children's school, but we all help.

3. We'll have a family meeting at the first of each month and decide together who should do which jobs. Once we have agreed, we'll be sure we know *how* and *when* to do our jobs, and we won't complain about them all month.

Things improved for the Petersons, but they still needed several of this chapter's principles.

One morning I awoke to the sound of urgent voices and the clatter of pans. We were at my mother's house. The night before, Richard and I had spoken at a fireside near her home, and Mom had gladly consented to keep the children for us. I was roused from a deep sleep to hear Mom say in a rather urgent voice, "Shawni, don't just sit there—get this sweater on and come out and help us quick!"

What on earth could be wrong? By the time I pulled on my clothes and got to the kitchen, I could see that Mom had rousted three of the older children (ages nine, seven, and six) as well as their father out of bed at 6:00 A.M., and they were frantically picking beans in the garden.

I had been cold in the night, and it was still pretty chilly, so I huddled up in a nearby blanket. Mother has really flipped this time, I thought. My mom has a lot of pizzazz, and she has always been the most ambitious go-getter I have ever known. I could see that the children were shivering in the cold bean field, however, and wondered if she hadn't gone a little too far.

Within half an hour Richard plopped a huge bucket full of beans on the kitchen table, and the children came in with chattering teeth. Then my mother stormed in the door and announced, "I asked one of you to turn the water on for me out there, and you just walked off and left me." Silence hung over the children. They couldn't think of a thing to say.

"And I see that no one put the beans in the water either!" Another silence. We all knew that Grandma was mad!

"Who did you tell to put the beans in the water?" I asked to break the awkward silence, thinking I would really hand out a tongue lashing and relieve the tension.

"The daddy!" she said emphatically.

"Oh," I said, smiling out of the corner of my mouth at a chagrined father looking like a naughty little boy caught in the act.

"Why do you want those beans in the water?" I asked, knowing that was not our usual procedure for putting up beans.

"Don't you know? Didn't anyone tell you?" she asked. "It froze last night! If we hadn't got those beans off the vines before the sun hit them, they would certainly be ruined!" She continued, "Sometimes if you put water on frozen plants before they warm up, they can be saved."

Suddenly I understood her urgency. The lovely crop of beans she had so carefully planted, weeded, and nurtured all summer long, mostly for our benefit, looked as if it would be totally destroyed because of one cruel, early summer frost. Why hadn't I thought of that? Being away from farm life for many years had dimmed my memory of the horror of the early frosts for which Bear Lake was notorious.

"Well, it looks like you've saved this many anyway," I said, trying to think of something encouraging to say.

"Maybe," she ventured, not yet ready to be too optimistic. She was still upset—primarily at the weather, but also at the children.

Before long, things calmed down a bit and Saren, Shawni, Saydi, Mom, and I settled down to snap beans.

"What children really need to be taught is how to work," Grandma said in her most tactful way. Her statement went right to my very soul. "They need to be taught that work needs to be done whether they like it or not." I wondered how much complaining took place in the bean patch, as she concluded, "And they need to be taught to follow through to the end and not just leave loose ends hanging!"

My life seemed to flash before my eyes, and I remembered the many times she had tried to instill that in me when I was growing up.

With snapping beans as background music, she proceeded to tell us about the time when her father had told her to drive a buckrake from one field to another, a chore that required passing over a narrow path bordered on one side by a cliff and on the other by a deep ravine. She was about twelve years old at the time.

"If I had measured, I'm sure there wouldn't have been an inch left over on either side," she said. "But I did it without question, though I was scared to death. I knew that if the rake started to fall, the horse and I would go with it," she explained with great expression and drama.

"Why, when my brother and sister and I were six, seven, and eight, we were put in a big box my dad had made for us on the harrow so we wouldn't fall out, and he left us, with our little lunch bags, to harrow the fields for the day. He left us at dawn and picked us up at dusk." The girls' mouths seemed to fall a little wider open at each successive story.

By the time we finished snapping the beans, the children

had a new appreciation for their grandmother. Something else very interesting happened too. After the beans, we put up a bushel of pears, and the children worked like little troopers. There was not one complaint! Occasionally we sent them off to play while we got the next project organized. The minute we called them, they were there with willing hands. I could hardly believe what a great day we had and what a sense of satisfaction the children felt when they showed their father the fruit of their labors at the end of the day.

As the day progressed, Mom and I had a chance to talk a lot about the responsibility of work. She pointed out the many advantages of farm living in teaching children to work. Having taught school for forty years, she said that she could usually tell those children who had lived on farms because of how they tackled their schoolwork.

Knowing that my children would probably never have the opportunity for full-time farm experience, I wondered if I would ever be able to teach them responsibility. However, as I thought further about it, I realized that that was not totally true. Some things are easier to teach on a farm, but others are more easily taught elsewhere.

Therefore, in this chapter we will talk about ways and means to teach responsibility for work regardless of circumstances. We hope some of these ideas fit into your family so that you too can nurture happy children who understand and appreciate the value of work. Incidentally, as evidenced by the previous story, we hope it helps us, too!

B. Methods

1. *Whistle while you work.* (To implant the idea that work can be fun, and that the fulfillment that comes from it is always fun.)

Everyone remembers Tom Sawyer, who made the job of whitewashing a fence appear so attractive that other boys paid him to do part of it. The interesting thing about that story is that the boys enjoyed it. They didn't just imagine that it was fun—it actually was fun, because of their attitude.

Small children whose parents enjoy work will accept the responsibilities of work naturally, and even with a degree of ease.

Make a conscious effort to reveal to your children the fulfilling side of work. Tell them how good it feels to get a job done. Tell them how glad you are to have the strength or ability to do a certain job. And yes, if you can bring yourself to do it, sing or whistle while you work.

2. *Family institution meeting.* (To help children see the scope of work in a household and to feel the honor of sharing in that work.)

Announce at least a week ahead of time that there will be a special family meeting for everyone old enough to read (probably six and up).

At the meeting, begin by telling the children how much you love them and want to make home a warm and wonderful place for them to live and grow. Then show them a list of the things that have to be done to keep home a pleasant place. The list should be big and readable. It might look something like this:

Do shopping	Do laundry
Prepare meals	Fix broken things
Do dishes	Drive people places
Clean house	Prepare Church assignments
Vacuum	Feed pets
Wash windows	Turn off lights
Pick up clutter	Empty dishwasher
Make beds	Set table
Clean bathrooms	Empty garbage and trash
Clean and wax floor	
Maintain outside	
Mow lawn	
Shovel snow	
Trim bushes	
Water lawn	
Care for garden	
Wash car	

Then, in your own words and on a level your children can understand, convey the following ideas: "These jobs are very important because doing them well makes our house a good home. When children are little babies, they aren't old enough to help. But as they get bigger, they are smart enough and strong enough to start doing some of these important things. Which things do you think you are big enough to do?"

Aim your discussion at connecting certain children with certain jobs. Put names by the jobs. There will be four keys to your success:

(a) *Keep it simple.* It is usually better if each child has one or two basic daily jobs and one or two basic weekly jobs. He won't do them if he can't remember them.

(b) Be sure each child knows exactly *how* to do his job. Do it *with* him several times. Show him the finer points. Show him how to take pride in doing it right. He won't do it if he doesn't think he knows how.

(c) *Follow through.* Be sure each child does his assignments every day and every week. Habits take a month or two to develop, and every time he fails to do a job, the habit-forming process is set back almost to day one. He won't do it if he doesn't think you'll follow through.

(d) *Make it visible.* Prepare a chart that shows the child's name and his job and that is marked each time he completes the job. (Colored stars may be the easiest and most effective mark.) He won't do it unless he gets reinforcement for it.

Children younger than six can, of course, have little family jobs of their own, but usually do not understand or relate well to this kind of a discussion.

3. *Ancestor stories.* (To help children see that their ancestors had to work much harder than most people today, and that working was good, and often fun, for them.)

If you have journals or records of your parents or grandparents, and if you can find or remember incidents in their lives involving work, then you may have a powerful opportunity to pass on to your children not only the theory but also the tradition of work.

Tell the incident to your children in simple language. Be sure they understand exactly whom you are talking about and that they are descendants, and therefore part of that ancestor.

Follow the story with a discussion of the importance and joy of work. You may want to write down the stories you use so that they can be retold periodically.

4. *Take the day off.* (To show children how fast a household can deteriorate when the work isn't done.)

When you have established a clearly defined pattern of family jobs, try this method to impress children with how important all of the jobs are. Pick a Saturday when the children's "weekly jobs" are usually performed; try to choose a day when most of the family will be home for most of the day. Be prepared for a fairly frazzling experience but one that teaches a memorable lesson.

At dinner the night before, surprise the children by saying, "Let's not do any of our family jobs tomorrow. We're tired, let's just take the day off." You'll get some puzzled looks, and also some delighted looks.

Then play it straight and really do nothing the next day. Don't fix any meals or do any dishes; don't sweep any floors or wash any clothes. Tell the children not to wash their basins or empty the garbage, or whatever their regular jobs are. When a child wants food (babies excluded, of course), tell them in a friendly way to get their own, that no one is doing any work today.

By evening you'll have a good deal of distemper, some hungry children, a messy house, and a high level of chaos and confusion.

Gather the family together and ask them if they want to do the same thing the next week. They won't. Then have a discussion about the importance of family jobs. Starting with the parents, have each family member make a commitment to do his daily jobs each day and his weekly jobs each week without fail. Then get busy together and clean up the house for Sunday.

5. *Saturday job auction.* (To get children involved with work beyond their regular jobs, and to teach them the connections between work and rewards.)

Children should be motivated to do their regular jobs as a part of the family, as their fair share, and to gain natural satisfaction. However, it is also a good idea to teach them that many jobs are worth doing not only because they are important, but also because they pay.

Make a list of the things that need doing that are not regularly assigned jobs, and put a price by each of them (such as wax the downstairs floor, 75 cents; clean out work bench drawer, 50 cents; and so forth.) Let the children take turns choosing a job. If a child doesn't want to participate, don't force him. Help him see the difference between regular jobs, which are his responsibility, and optional jobs, which he can do if he wants to earn money. If your children have gained the responsibility for money, as discussed in the last chapter, you'll find that very few jobs will go unclaimed.

Be sure children are paid quickly after they complete a job, either in cash or by credit entry to their "family bank book" (described in the previous chapter). For some jobs a time limit is helpful; for others it is wise to take more time and do the job with precision and pride, emphasizing the satisfaction of quality rather than speed or quantity.

Just a word about rewards. Our Father in heaven always uses this principle! Every good act we perform is rewarded with some kind of blessing. Even a secret good deed is rewarded by an inner sense of satisfaction in having done a good deed.

The reward for completing regular family jobs and responsibilities should be the simple satisfaction of having done a good job, with perhaps the enhancement of a star on a chart or a peg in a pegboard. However, performing other kinds of work can be rewarded monetarily or materially.

Small children find it difficult to understand anything except immediate rewards (even a smile of approval is a great reward). *As children grow older, however, they begin to understand the principle of long-range rewards as well as immediate ones, such as performing in an orchestra because they practiced hard.*

Rewards are not only acceptable in a family working together to improve—they are essential!

6. *Build something together.* (To reinforce the pleasure of work by sharing it and putting children close to your example.)

The summer I was ten, my father and brother and I built a log cabin in the mountains. We cut the trees, notched the logs, split the shingles, and bricked the fireplace. My father loved the hard work. I loved it because he did. I've never forgotten the communication of that summer, both verbal and nonverbal.

Whether it's a cabin or a doghouse or just finishing a room in the basement, building together is a constructive and valuable endeavor, one that creates in children an honest desire for the responsibility of work.

7. *Have a garden with assigned crops.* (To teach children the law of the harvest, which should be at the heart of their understanding of the responsibility of work.)

While I was a mission president, I was amused and amazed at how easy it was to pick out missionaries who had been raised on farms. Almost without exception they started out more responsible than their city counterparts. A farm environment not only demands a great deal of hard work; it also teaches the invaluable law of the harvest—that one reaps only what he sows. A farm or garden may not be the only way to teach this lesson, but it is probably the most direct and effective way to teach it.

If it is possible, arrange to have a garden. Give each child a plot. Decide together which child will raise which vegetable. It is simpler and often more effective when each child has only one crop.

Tell the children you will help them, and answer their

questions when they ask, but help them understand that they are responsible for their own garden. Then stick with it. Remind them once in a while when watering or weeding is needed, but don't push them. Let the law of the harvest work.

When they do harvest, help them see that they could have had more if they'd worked harder, and less if they had not worked as hard.

C. Family Focal Point: The Peg Board

As in so many families, our family chores and the efforts we made to get certain procedures incorporated on a day-to-day basis were mixed successes. Sometimes they seemed to work brilliantly; other times they seemed to be total failures.

We did at one point, however, chance upon a practice that has eliminated this erratic pattern and replaced it with fairly consistent efforts by all of the children to do their part. We think it has also helped them to feel the joy as well as the responsibility of purposeful work.

We had been using a system where the child got a star on the "chore chart" each time he did his job. When he got twenty stars, he was given a reward. What we began to notice was that the reward wasn't really necessary. The *stars* were what the children wanted. The stars were the reward. They wanted the satisfaction of putting a bright star on the chart by their name. The star symbolized accomplishment, fulfillment, the completion of a task.

That started us thinking. If it was the act of putting on that star that motivated them, how could we expand that motivation by offering them something like a star, only bigger and better. What we came up with was a peg board. It consists of a two-by-four board (about 14 inches in length) for each child. The boards have four half-inch holes in them, and four big, blocky wooden pegs are attached to the board with string. Each child's two-by-four has his name carved on it and is attached to the others with dowels. The whole effect looks something like this:

Each peg represents one responsibility that the children have each day and can be pushed into its hole only when that responsibility is fulfilled. In our case the first peg is the "morning peg" and can go in when the child has made his bed, brushed his teeth, and had his morning prayer. The second peg is the "practice peg"; it can go in when the child has done his one hour (half an hour for smaller ones) of music practice for the day. The third peg is the "job peg"; it goes in when the child's daily job is done. The last peg is the "evening peg"; it can go in when the child has put his things away, has laid his clothes out for the next school day, and has said his evening prayer.

All the jobs can be done before dinner, so it is standard procedure that all pegs must be in place before a child eats (the evening peg is from the evening before).

The interesting thing is that the chief motivation for getting the pegs in is not the threat of having no dinner; it is the satisfaction of the pegs themselves and what they represent. They are big and blocky, and they fit snugly into their holes. It's fun to put them in and fun to look at them after they are in. The children receive praise each evening when they put the last ones in, and they feel good about having taken care of their responsibilities that day.

Whether you use pegs, stars, or something similar, this visual family focal point can go a long way toward promoting consistency in your children's acceptance of the responsibility of work.

As parents in a modern society, we often don't realize the benefits of work for our children. We think we are doing them a big favor by doing things for them. We consider them either too young for the responsibility or too old to be bothered with little jobs.

I was making my three-year-old's bed one day, and thinking that she should be making it. Recalling the struggle I had experienced in urging her to make her own bed, I finally decided that it just wasn't worth it to try again. I would make the bed myself. I decided that she was too little and would "grow into it."

I realized later that that decision was probably wrong. Children at ages three and four have a real need to feel responsible. They thrive on responsibility and feel great satisfaction in the doing if they are properly taught how. Too often we tell children to do things we have done many times, and when they don't do them, we fail to realize that it may be because they don't know how.

I recall a conversation with a friend whom I considered to be one of the most responsible people I had ever met. When I asked him about his youth as an only child, he told me that he could not remember being told to do something without help from his mother to accomplish it. It was never, "Go make your bed." It was always, "Let's go make your bed." He learned responsibility as his mother taught him how to do things.

I had only three children at that time, but even then I thought, That's fine for an only child, but what about mothers who have troops of children? *Making a bed with each child each day didn't seem any more feasible than having a platoon sergeant help each soldier to make his bed each day.*

As we had more children, however, I realized that it is not only possible, but absolutely crucial to help little children learn how. It is possible to take time after the older children are off to school to give pointers on things like making beds or cleaning rooms. It helps to remember that we have to accept pretty lumpy beds even at that. I've learned to ask my two-year-old if his bed is made before I pass judgment.

The next step is to encourage children to do what they know how to do on a regular basis on their own initiative. After trying many things that didn't work, we decided to have them set their own goals concerning making their beds, cleaning their rooms, and brushing their teeth. I remember when our four-year-old decided that he wanted to make his bed every day for his weekly goal. For four days out of seven I went into his room in the morning to find, to my amazement, that his bed was already made. On the other three days a few words to remind him brought immediate results. When I think of all the struggles we have had with children through the years, I am amazed that it took me so long to figure out how to get results: first, teach them how; then, let them set the goal.

The same principles apply with slightly older children. Since I try to teach several of ours a music lesson each day before school, one of our dilemmas was how to get breakfast prepared at the same time. The only two children not involved in music lessons at the time were the six- and seven-year-olds. One Saturday I spent a couple of hours teaching them how to prepare various breakfast foods. Since then, we've never eaten better. They prepare breakfast every morning. They are much more creative than I am. Their creations are usually very good, and though we all crunch down on an eggshell occasionally, everybody's happy. There's almost nothing those children would rather do than create breakfast!

As children grow older, we assume that they have so many outside responsibilities (homework, ballet lessons, piano practice, Girl Scouts, and so forth) that they can't handle any home responsibilities. Often our natural inclination is to think, "I'll do the cooking, dishes, cleaning, and straighten their rooms for them, and leave them to the important things." In the long run, this is the wrong course.

Children should understand that mothers also have many responsibilities. They should know that she too has things that she likes to do to improve herself. When there is routine work to be done, everyone should share the responsibility.

It's extremely important for the father to be a part of this understanding and to "rally others to the cause." If he leads the children by willingly and cheerfully helping with dishes and other household chores, then the children will offer far less resistance themselves.

SECTION II

RESPONSIBILITY TO GOD (STEWARDSHIP)

Who are you?

For each of us there are many answers to that question. I knew a man who answered it in a hundred ways: His first answer was his name; then he listed a father, an engineer, a sailor, a husband, a tennis player, an amateur photographer, an American, a Christian, and so forth. His list was random, and it was easy to get to one hundred—any of us could.

However, in the *gospel* sense, the question has (and needs) only two answers: (1) We are children of God. (2) We are stewards. The second answer incorporates any additional answers we might think of. We are stewards over our bodies, over the earth, over our talents and our personalities, over our children. None of these belong to us. All are stewardships. If we are wise and good stewards, then one day stewardship will give way to ownership.

Responsibility takes on new meaning for parents who understand their stewardship to God. For one thing, the responsibility for children becomes awesome. Until this earth, we had played no role other than that of child, and the only parent was God. Now, here, he gives us the incredible opportunity of assuming his role—that of a parent—and of accepting the responsibility to parent and nurture others of his children, our brothers and sisters. It is, at once, both frightening and exhilarating to realize that God gives His children the high-risk gift of agency and sends them down without memory, and with only weak, mortal parents as their guide and stay.

In our stewardship over God's children, we need to operate on His timetable. He tells us clearly that eight years is the age of accountability. This is a dramatic and precise bequest of responsibility. When a child emerges from the waters of baptism, he is accountable and responsible to God. Teaching a child the nature and importance of that responsibility must start before age eight, and must continue long thereafter.

As mentioned earlier, in order to be meaningful, responsibility must be *to* someone. When it is, and when that someone is *real*, it becomes natural and in some ways almost easy to be responsible. Children should have the right and the pleasure of knowing that they are responsible for many wonderful things to a loving, but firm and demanding, Father—God.

The feeling of responsibility to God comes largely through awareness that He made us, that His Son died for us. Children can understand these simple facts; they can learn that God expects certain things of them, and that they are servants and stewards to God as well as His children. They can thus become responsible to God and gain the exaltation that full acceptance of that responsibility carries with it.

Acceptance of any kind of responsibility arises through motivation—either love or fear (or a combination of both). If we accept a civic responsibility, our motivation is usually a love for our community, or a fear of what could happen to it if that particular job didn't get done. If we are responsible in our jobs, it is because we fear losing them or love having them, or love the things the jobs let us have. If we are responsible parents, it is because we love our children and perhaps fear the consequences of not being good parents. We accept many responsibilities because of the pride we take in ourselves and our self-images as responsible people.

We usually think of *fear* as a negative word and *love* as a positive one, and in general, that is what they are. Love, however, can be negative and fear can be positive. It depends on the nature and the object of the love or fear. Love of material things produces negative consequences. Fear of God produces positive consequences.

The first great commandment is to love God. (Matthew 22:37.) At the same time, God describes His "jewels" as "those who fear him." (3 Nephi 24:16-

17.) It is those who fear Him that God has mercy on (Luke 12:5), and Abraham's greatness was a product of his fear of God (Genesis 22:12). The Lord even tells Moses that fear of God is what can help us to teach our children properly. (Deuteronomy 4:10.) As parents, we should do all we can to rid our children of most of their fears, but as we do so, let us allow the right kind of positive fear to remain.

The proper combinations of love and fear are the keys to teaching children responsibility. When love and the positive form of fear are combined, they produce respect, and respect yields responsibility. Children will become truly responsible to parents only when they both love and fear them—fear their disapproval *because* they love them, and fear the consequences that consistent parents will provide for nonresponsibility. Children will become responsible to themselves only as they both love and fear themselves—fear their potential to hurt others and fear missing their opportunities and potential.

But the most profound application of

the combination of love and fear is in this section. All of *God's* children, including us, will become genuinely responsible to God only when we both love and fear Him. Loving Him shows that we understand His overwhelming love for us and His mercy and atonement. Fearing Him shows that we understand His consistency, His absolute standards, His intolerance of any evil. His love for us is unconditional. His displeasure with sin is equally unconditional. One should produce love in us; the other, fear. Together they should become awe and respect. Publicus Lentulus, in a document purported to be an eye-witness account of Christ, described Him as having a countenance we may "both love and fear."

The challenge before us as parents is to be sure our children's fear of God is a product of their love for Him. Think about that. It must be that way and not the other way around. If children fear God because they love Him and know of His greatness and perfection, they will deeply want to be responsible to Him. Helping them to feel that way is the objective of this section.

Responsibility for Actions
... from behavior to repentance
7

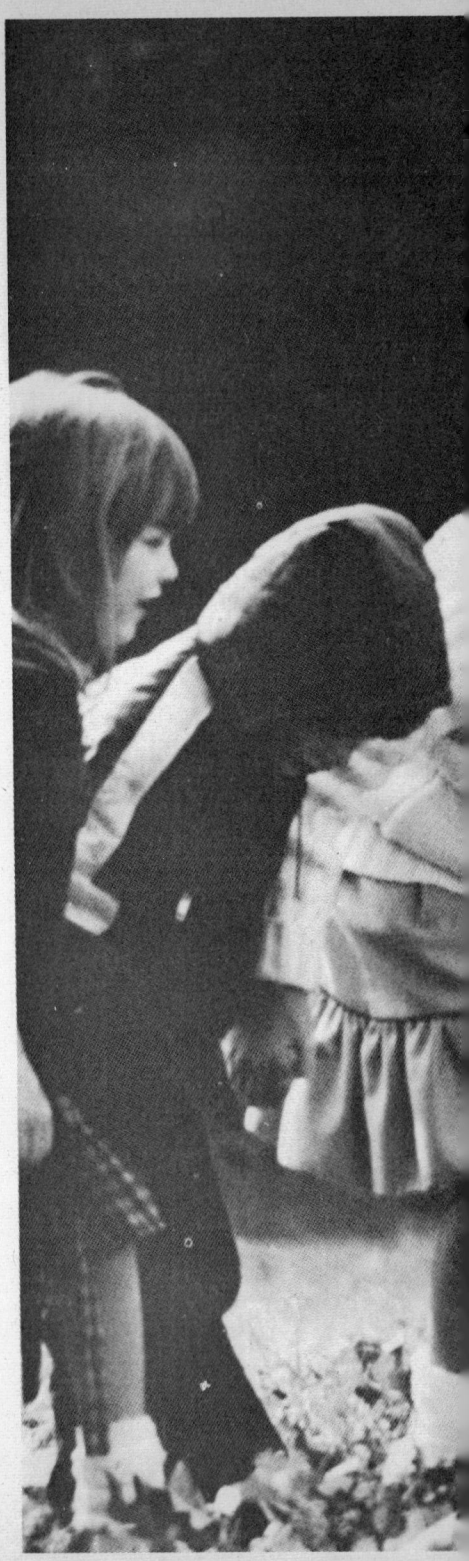

In the final analysis, the great need in the world is not for more genius, or even for more skill. It is for people willing to accept responsibility for what they do.

A. Definition and Illustration

"Ahhh!" some of you will say. "Now we're getting down to it—it's their *actions* that I want my children to be responsible for."

As parents, we usually think in the context of making our children responsible to *us* for their actions, and, to a degree, this is as it should be. Over the long term, however, the real key is to help them see (and to help ourselves to see) that it is really God to whom they are responsible, that from their baptism on, they are accountable to Him for all of their actions.

Helping them to see that, to feel that, and to love Heavenly Father enough to want to be responsible to Him for all that they do is the objective of the ideas discussed in this chapter.

Jason was seven. Just over the six-foot fence in his backyard was a parking lot for an apartment complex. Someone in that parking lot had tossed a paper bag of empty beer bottles over the fence, and Jason found them. For several reasons, not all of which he understood, he took the bottles and tossed them, one by one, back over the fence. Since he couldn't see through the fence, he couldn't see them land. But he could hear the crash, and the whole thing was kind of fun.

That evening a man from the apartment complex rang the doorbell, and Jason, who was downstairs, overheard the man telling his father about a punctured tire. Jason went quietly into his room, put on his pajamas, got in bed, and pretended very hard to be asleep.

His parents, after reassuring the neighbor that they would pay for the tire if it turned out to be their son's doing, sat down to decide how to handle the incident. They realized that they had three challenges: (1) to help Jason tell the truth about the matter (they knew him well enough to be pretty sure of what the truth was); (2) to help him repent of what he'd done; and (3) to help him feel enough responsibility for his actions that he wouldn't do something similarly irresponsible in the future. As they thought about it, they realized that it was fortunate that the whole thing had come to their attention after Jason was in bed, when they had time to think it through, rather than while he was still up. Otherwise they might have confronted him without much thought as to how to make it a learning experience.

When Jason came to breakfast the next morning, Dad said, "Son, I noticed that sack of beer bottles. Whoever tossed them into our yard shouldn't have done it, should he."

Jason looked up with a little hope in his eyes and said, "No."

Dad said, "You probably felt like tossing them back over and didn't really stop to think that they might hurt anyone or break something." Jason looked down, but said nothing. "Did you throw them over, son?"

There was a pause, then a quiet, "Yes."

"We're proud of you for telling the truth, son. A man's car ran over one of those bottles and got a flat tire. We're lucky none of the bottles broke a windshield. But we do need to figure out what to do about the flat tire." Dad's arm was around Jason's shoulders now. "Do you feel that you understand what repentance is?"

"Sort of."

"What is it, son?"

"It's when you're sorry."

"That's part of it. Do you feel sorry about throwing those bottles and puncturing the tire?"

"Yes."

"Well, I'll tell you something, Jason. Repentance is a magic kind of thing. When someone breaks a law or does something wrong, he has to have a punishment unless he repents. Repenting is being sorry and then making things right again and obtaining forgiveness from others and from God. If someone repents completely, he doesn't need a punishment. Would you like to try repentance?"

"Yes."

To cut a long story short, Jason cleaned up the rest of the glass. He saved money from odd jobs for three weeks to pay for the tire. He asked for and received forgiveness from the car's owner. He promised both his parents and the car owner that he would never throw anything over the fence again. He asked Heavenly Father to forgive him too.

The repentance process made a far stronger impression on Jason than a punishment would have. By making restitution, he gained the satisfaction of putting things right and the realization that putting things back together is usually much harder than breaking them.

The result was an increase in maturity and in Jason's general sense of responsibility for his actions.

Every child has some bad habits and mannerisms that we parents dislike intensely. Interestingly, children usually don't like these particular behavior aspects in themselves any better than we do. If you ask a child what his biggest behavior problem is, he will usually come up with the same conclusion you have.

One of our children thrives on being obedient, following the rules, and carrying out her responsibilities. Her problem is that she seems to lay in wait for the brother or sister who doesn't measure up. Two or three times a day she puts on a scowl and complains bitterly, incessantly, annoyingly, and loudly.

Another child cannot accept constructive criticism in any form. If she suspects that we think she has done something wrong, she sulks and stomps off to cry, (especially when she really has done something silly and she knows it.)

Three things can be done about these kinds of behavior

problems: *(1) Ignore them and hope they go away. (2) Accept the fact that your child is just "that way" and you'll just have to grin and bear it. (3) Communicate your concerns and sit down together to work out a way for the child to change his actions and for parents to change their responses. Of course, the third solution is essential, yet many of us use the first or second instead.*

We must first identify the problem and then work out a solution that child and parent can work on together. Once children are taught basic principles, they should then be taught that the responsibility for their actions is truly theirs, not ours. We are simply there to help.

Our challenge is to teach children how to cope with actions that are a problem, how to control their anger, and how to handle success and failure. Once they have these tools, we must let them take the responsibility for solutions to problems regarding their actions. Our tendency is to demand our own solutions arbitrarily and without consultation. When children decide what they themselves want their actions to be, the result is miraculous.

B. Methods

1. *Laws.* (To help children realize that God's laws are simply loving counsel from a wise Father.)

The "family laws" discussed in the obedience chapter are a good starting point in helping children to feel responsible for their actions. Take your family laws chart and place it next to a poster or paper listing the Ten Commandments. Assemble the children and conduct this kind of a dialogue:

"What do we call *these* laws?" (Family laws.)

"Who gave them to us?" (You, our parents.)

"Why did we make them?" (Because you love us, and you know that our family will be happier if we keep those laws.)

"Who tries to make sure you live them and don't break them?" (You.)

"Now, whose laws are *these*?" (Heavenly Father's.)

"Why does he give them to us?" (He loves us, and living them will make us happy.)

"How many fathers do we have?" (Two.)

"Where are they?" (One is here, and one is up in heaven.)

"Do they both give you laws?" (Yes.)

"Why?" (They both love us, and laws make us happier.)

"If you had parents who didn't love you and didn't care what you did, would they give you laws?" (No.)

Then go through the Ten Commandments together and talk about how keeping each one brings happiness, and how breaking each one brings unhappiness. Talk about other counsel and laws God has given us, and about how each one is a way to be happy.

2. *Positive reinforcement.* (To strengthen children's tendencies toward honesty and appropriate actions through the sheer weight of the attention and positive recognition it brings them.)

While it may be too general to call a technique, reinforcement is the most powerful means that parents have to develop a feeling of responsibility for actions within their children. Praise every incident of honesty, of politeness, of sharing, of good decision-making. Make the praise direct and clear. Look the child in the eyes and tell him how proud you are of that action. Then take the compliment beyond that one incident by telling him that he is *that kind of person* ("You are a very honest boy." "You remember to say thank you so much better than you did last year," and so forth.)

If there is one simple and profoundly important truth about children, it is that they live up to their reputations. They will do what they think is actually expected of them. If you can control what *they* think *you* think of them, you can control their actions.

3. *Five-facet review.* (To pinpoint in advance the kinds of behavior problems individual children are likely to be most susceptible to.)

As a part of the "five-facet review" (discussed in more detail in chapter 8), take time to discuss the behavioral problems of each child. This is a good way to begin the five-facet review. Then, as you review the physical, mental, emotional, social, and spiritual progress of each child, you may well discover some of the reasons or sources of the behavior problems.

The beauty of this approach is the fact that recognizing a behavior problem, defining it, and finding its source go a long way toward solving it.

4. *The conscience-and-consequence game.* (To help children realize that there really is a "still small voice" that will tell them what is right, if they are good listeners, and to show them that doing what is right always pays off in the long run.)

Prepare in advance some simple three-by-five-inch index cards with certain dilemmas on one side and the long-term consequences of the choice on the other side. For example, here are two typical dilemmas:

Card 1	Card 2
Look across the aisle to Susan's desk and copy her test answers.	Don't cheat; just do your own best on the test. Prepare better next time.
Get an A on the test.	Get a D on the test, so your parents are mad at you.

Have the child who is "it" pick one option card or the other. Before he does, however, have another child represent his conscience, or the Holy Ghost, and whisper in his ear that he should take the *right* one.

When the cards are turned over, they reveal the long-term consequences of each decision.

Card 1	Card 2
You will never learn much in school. You will always do badly on tests where you can't cheat. You will get caught sometimes, and people will know that you cheat. Your only friends are other people who cheat.	You will study harder and do better on the next test. People will trust you, and you will like yourself.

Other examples of cards follow. You will want to come up with some of your own that fit closely with the actual concerns and potential behavior problems of your own children.

Card 1	Card 2
Lie in bed a little longer. It's cold and you're tired. Mom thinks you're sick and lets you stay home from school.	Get right up and get your school things together. You do your household jobs and get right off to school on time.

Card 1	Card 2
You have a lazy day where you don't learn much of anything. You feel like a lazy person who never gets much done.	Your actions make for a happy, alert day where you learn a lot and feel good.

Actions

Card 1

Try the cigarette Bobby has. The other kids pat you on the back and think you're neat.

Card 2

Tell Bobby you would never smoke a cigarette and don't think that he should either. The other kids call you a chicken and tell you to "get lost."

Card 1

No one really respects you because you're afraid to stand up for what you believe. When you get older you become a smoker and don't feel like coming to church anymore.

Card 2

Kids start to look up to you because you do what is right. Some of *them* decide not to smoke anymore because they want to follow your example.

Card 1

Don't tell your mother that you ate the cookies. She blames your little sister, and you get away with the lie.

Card 2

Tell her you ate them, and you're sorry, and you'll not do it again. Mom makes *you* make more cookies.

Card 1

No one trusts you because you tell lies.

Card 2

People want you for a friend because they trust you.

Card 1	Card 2
Ignore the old lady who needs the snow shoveled Go skiing instead.	Go and shovel her sidewalks. You miss a great ski trip.
Card 1	Card 2
You become a selfish person who always thinks of himself and never of others. The only friends you have are the ones who want something from you.	You learn the joy of service. You serve others and find that others serve you and love you.

Discuss with your children how the short-term consequences of the wrong choice usually seems pretty good, but that the long-term consequences always catch up with you.

5. *Teach vertical and horizontal vision.* (To help children envision the very real purposes and consequences of their lives and their actions.)

Designate a particular *place* somewhere in the home where you can gather the children for especially important discussions about important things—around the dining room table, on a certain couch, in the den. It should be thought of as a place where you take them to talk about weighty matters—a teaching station, as it were.

At the teaching station, review with them where we were before birth and where we will go after death. Depending on their ages, their Sunday School or Primary teachers, and your own previous teaching, they will know parts of the plan of salvation, but review it as a "horizontal" passage through time, starting with Heavenly Father, coming here to learn to be responsible and choose the right, and going back to Him in His celestial kingdom. The central theme should be that Heavenly Father sent us down to learn how to do good and choose right without having to have someone force us or tell us all the time, so that we can be more like Him and live with Him again.

Then try to expand their "vertical" vision. Read to them what Joseph Smith saw regarding the celestial kingdom and outer darkness in Doctrine and Covenants 76, or tell it in your own words. Ask the children which place they want to end up in. Ask them what it takes to go to the best place. Be sure they really internalize the answer of being responsible for their actions. If they are eight or older, be sure they understand accountability and that any wrong action not repented of can become a barrier to the celestial kingdom.

6. *Two kinds of mistakes.* (To help slightly older children grasp the idea of commission and omission, to help them feel responsible not only for *not* doing wrong things, but for *doing* more right things.)

Tell, in your own words, the following story:

Bill had the worst day of his life. He was called to the principal's office twice in one day.

The first time was in the morning. Tommy had brought a pair of pliers to school, and he and Bill took the bolts out of the teeter-totter at recess just before two little girls sat on it. The teeter-totter came apart, and the girls skinned their knees. The principal gave them a lecture they would never forget. He said, "Bill, there are certain things you must *not* do!"

Then that afternoon, Bill was called in again. This time it was because he hadn't done his math homework all week. The principal said, "Bill, there are certain things you *must* do!"

Have a discussion with the children about the two kinds of sins—one is "doing wrong things," the other is "not doing right things." Give them several examples of sins or mistakes, and see if they can determine which category they fit. You might use the "wrong choice" cards from the consequence game (method 4 in this chapter).

7. *Erasing the black marks.* (To simplify the concept of repentance and to show how it applies to sins of commission and to sins of omission.)

On a sheet of lined paper, write two or three random names. (Be sure they are not the names of children whom your children know.) Then, using the "wrong choice" cards from the consequence game, connect a mistake with one of the names on your sheet of paper (for example, Julie looked on someone else's paper and cheated on a test). With a soft pencil, make a black mark by Julie's name. Then say:

"Julie made a mistake. Which kind of mistake was it—doing something wrong, or not doing something right? When we make mistakes, it's as though we are given a black mark. Heavenly Father says we have to repent of our sins before we can go back and live with Him. Repenting is like erasing the black mark. How can Julie repent of cheating?" (She can tell her teacher what she did and that she doesn't deserve the A. She can ask forgiveness from her teacher and from Heavenly Father and promise never to do it again.) "If she did all that, her black mark would be erased."

Erase Julie's black mark and repeat the process with one of the other names and one of the other "wrong choice" cards. Each time be sure the children understand that repentance is difficult and often embarrassing, but that one feels so much better inside afterwards. Be sure each individual discussion of "what would she have to do to repent" includes confessing and apologizing, making restitution, and asking forgiveness and promising not to do it again.

Help the children to see that by trying very hard to avoid both kinds of sin and by repenting whenever we make mistakes, we can keep the black marks off and thus feel happy inside and be able to go back and live with Heavenly Father someday.

8. *Efforts to connect repentance with gratitude and with the Atonement.* (To help older children begin to appreciate and comprehend what Christ has done for us.)

(a) Read The Chronicles of Narnia *by C. S. Lewis.* Lewis's

great series of seven books for children can help you teach relatively young children certain principles of Christianity that might otherwise be beyond their level of comprehension. Through the Christ-figure of a great lion and through a wide range of connected stories of rich and serene symbolism, Lewis weaves a framework in which children can grasp the concepts of justice and mercy, of repentance and atonement, and, most of all, of personal love and awe for the Lord. Once you start the Chronicles, be prepared for a lot of nights of reading and a lot of children's pleas for "just one more chapter."

(b) *The reason we can repent is Jesus.* Tell your children a simple story about a man who broke a law. The judge told him he would either have to pay a fine or go to jail. The man didn't have nearly enough money to pay the fine. He told the judge that he was very sorry, but the judge said he'd still have to go to jail unless he paid the fine. Then the man's older brother came along. He had much more money, and he paid the fine so that his little brother did not have to go to jail.

Explain to the children in simple terms that when we make mistakes and break God's laws, we have to pay for them by being punished. Otherwise we might have to go and live somewhere else and *not* be with Heavenly Father. Explain that even when we say we're sorry, we can't pay the full fine. Give your testimony that our elder Brother, Jesus, took the punishment for us when He died on the cross. Talk about all of this in the context of how much we love Him, how much we owe Him, how grateful we are to Him, and how much we want to live the laws He gives us.

You may find it interesting to try this type of discussion with your children both before and after you read them "The Lion, the Witch, and the Wardrobe," the first in Lewis's *Narnia* series.

Once again, the secret to success in teaching our children to act in a certain way or to change their actions is our own consistency.

A simple illustration comes to mind. One of the most impressive traits about British children is their consistent habit of saying "please" and "thank you." During the three years our family spent in England, I seldom heard a child ask for or receive anything without a "please" or "thank you." When there was a rare miss, the parent always delivered a gentle reminder. Courtesy is a national tradition.

Sentences begin with "please." "Please may I have more milk?" Likewise, a thank-you is given after each small service. A little friend never left our door after an afternoon at play without saying, "Thank you for having me."

In contrast, I recently took nineteen American children, ranging in age from one to ten, in our van to a pumpkin patch to pick their own Halloween pumpkins. The trip took half an hour each way. The children had a wonderful time, but by the time we returned with nineteen kids and nineteen pumpkins, we were all happy to scramble out! The trip had taken considerable time that I could have used to do other things. My baby was screaming, hungry, and miserable all the way home, and my gas tank was seriously depleted. But not one child thought to say "thank you."

Unknowingly and unwittingly, we Americans teach our children to be what the British would consider rude and selfish. Most of us would like our children to be polite, but perhaps we do not desire it enough to pay the price of consistency.

Children do exactly what is expected of them. We have had young women from England living with us for short periods of time on a couple of occasions. By the time they left to return home, our children were markedly more polite. However, as the reminders stopped, so did the children's habit of speaking more politely.

The lesson is a simple one—but by no means easy. Children's actions are changed only by regular reminders, consistent praise, and positive reinforcement.

C. Family Focal Points: "Bathroom Chats," Laws and Repentance, Code Words

Several years ago, while I was a graduate student and our oldest daughter was just beginning to talk, I wanted to begin regular, private, one-on-one "interviews" with her. Since our small student apartment had only one private room in it, these little meetings took on the title "bathroom chats." They have since become Sunday traditions (now occurring elsewhere, but still called "bathroom chats" by the older children). As mentioned in chapter 8, one purpose of the chats is to talk about each child's gifts and reinforce his individuality. As chapter 12 will discuss, it also creates a setting in which he or she may tell me about their monthly and weekly goals. The third objective of these private chats applies to this chapter.

What we do is to ask each child six or older what he thinks are the main things he needs to improve in. Amazingly, children usually know, and if the atmosphere of trust is right, they will bring up the very things you want them to. A child will say, "I need to be more careful to always tell the truth" or "I need to stop fighting with Saydi." How quickly he comes to his real problems depends partly on how well you have made him aware of them. But once he (through whatever hints and prods you need to give) identifies an area of need in himself, it becomes his goal to change it, with your help, rather than vice versa. The weekly (some say monthly is more realistic) repetitive nature of the individual chats allows follow-through and allows you to help your child see that it *is* possible to change and improve. I often put a "code letter" on the back of the child's hand (opposite the "gifts" represented on their fingers—see chapter 8). In this way they remember the behavior problem they are trying to correct. Also, because there is only *one* problem as opposed to *lots* of good things, they feel self-esteem and don't lose confidence because of the singular problem.

To get the needed individual behavior changes even more "out on the table," we sometimes devote a family meeting to letting each child tell the family what he has decided he needs to work hardest on. Other family members then encourage him, praise him for having the courage to say it, and promise to help.

This kind of individual attention to behavior is particularly important and appropriate with seven-year-olds, who should be consciously repenting in preparation for baptism.

Of course, the family laws are the heart of responsibility for actions. Family laws, properly used and enforced, can be a prototype or training ground for children's abilities to keep God's laws. Since the punishment-consequences of God's laws can be avoided through repentance, it should be likewise for our family laws. Our children know that, if they truly repent for violating a family law, they can escape its punishment (as long as it doesn't happen too often). It is thrilling to see a four-year-old who has hurt his little brother and taken a toy away from him go back, return the toy, put his arms around him, and say, "I'm sorry. Will you forgive me? I won't do that any more." Even your small children can reach a level where you can simply say, "Repent, Josh, or you will get the punishment for the family law you broke."

Often, all that children need is a quick and subtle reminder of the need to pay more attention to the correctness of their actions. We have developed some simple codes that we use as reminders in our family. They are particularly useful in situations where we are in someone else's home, or when others are in our home and a direct reminder might embarrass our children. When we want to remind them that their behavior is wrong in some way, we give them a "thumbs up" hand sign. When we want them to look around and see what needs doing, we give them the "OK" sign where thumb touches the pointer finger. This is an "eye" sign, which means, "look around and see what needs to be done here." We also have some verbal codes like, "Did you remember to send that letter?" This means there is someone here that you don't know, and you should get acquainted. When we get a child's attention and clear our throat, we mean "Remember your manners." Each family could develop its own signs and codes; children often respond better to subtle reminders than to major, overt corrections.

If some of the teaching methods in this chapter help your children feel a sense of responsibility to God for their actions and understand that true repentance is an "eraser," your family will then be in a position where some form of regular behavior review, coupled with some code words and an ongoing repentance process, will build genuine responsibility for actions into the characters of your children.

Responsibility for Gifts ... from earth and body to talents

8

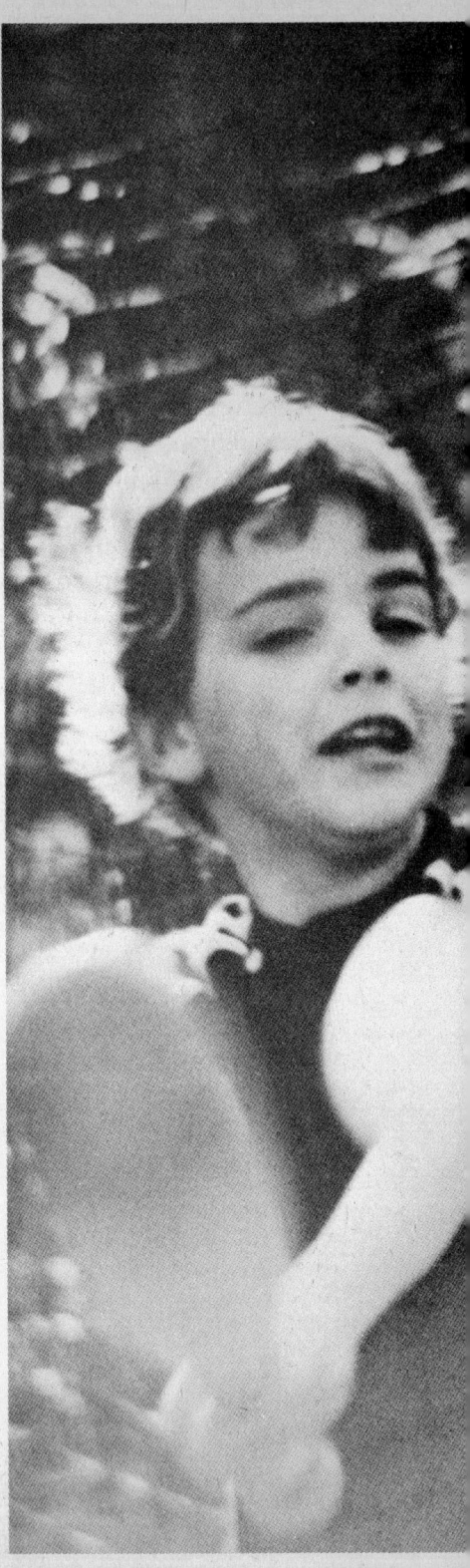

The best things in life are free, simply because they are gifts from a wise and loving Heavenly Father.

A. Definition and Illustration

Gifts!

The word conjures images of packages tied with ribbons on birthdays or at Christmas. But how much more the word can mean—gifts from God!

The best things in life are free, simply because they are gifts from a loving Father. The sky, our bodies, the plants that grow, our abilities and talents—these are just the start of an endless list of gifts from God. God's gifts are both a loan and a test—a loan to our stewardship, and a test to see if we are responsible enough to keep them forever.

Mark was nine. For nearly six years his parents had been aware that he had exceptional conceptual and artistic gifts. When he was three, he could draw shapes and make numbers and letters with surprising accuracy. By the time he started school, he was drawing animals and trees that looked like the product of a child at least five years older. His parents arranged private art lessons for him that year. All went very well, and the praise and recognition that Mark's drawing brought him kept him motivated and happy.

Then a year ago, a couple of things happened. First, little-league soccer and baseball started. Then two or three of Mark's peers decided that drawing and art were for girls and sissies, and they voiced this opinion in many not-very-nice ways to Mark. The situation claimed everybody's attention one day when Mark came home from school and announced to his mother, first, that he was no longer an artist—he was a ballplayer, and second, that he didn't intend to draw anything again as long as he lived.

Meanwhile, as Mark's story was unfolding, another story was taking place in parallel. Mark's little brother Tommy, two years younger, had been living in Mark's shadow. While everyone had been exclaiming over Mark's obvious and visible talent, everyone was wondering just where Tommy's talent was. It was easier to see where Tommy's talents *weren't*. He certainly couldn't draw. He showed no particular musical or athletic aptitude, and his life had consisted mostly of looking for (and having others look for) some gift or ability to counterpart Mark's. It hadn't been found. Tommy was basically an average child who spent most of his spare time playing with the little girl and boy next door, ages three and two.

Mark's sudden announcement eventually became a blessing in disguise. It caused his parents, Bill and Marge Caine, to focus on the whole question of talents and/or the lack of them in both boys. After a long discussion, Bill summarized the problem to his wife. "Marge, it's simple—we have one untalented boy and one talented one who doesn't like his talent. We might be doing something right, but I'd hate to have to try and name it."

But the situation and the discussion represented a turning point. Both Bill and Marge began to think more directly about their responsibility to help their children discover what their attributes were, both the obvious and the nonobvious ones, and to help them gain a sense of their responsibility and opportunity to develop them.

In this frame of mind, they began to see Tommy in a new light. They recognized that he had several gifts that had not been apparent to them before. Among them was a rather remarkable ability to teach and influence small children. Tommy's "play" with the two children next door consisted mostly of teaching them little games and telling them stories. He had a beautiful and compassionate way with little children. They also noticed that Tommy had an exceptional ability to persevere. He could work at something much longer than Mark. He followed through. He didn't feel right until a thing was done. For a child, he was unusually dependable. He wasn't brilliant or quick at learning, but his attention span was long. He made up for his lack of quickness with his tenacity. It was through talking together about Tommy that his parents began to notice these qualities.

As they recognized them, they found themselves being more complimentary toward Tommy, praising him more, pointing out to him how good he was at certain things. Tommy flourished under the praise, and Mark started looking for ways to win back his old monopoly on his parents' compliments. He even started drawing again. The parents responded by redoubling the praise of Mark's talent. They took him to museums. They checked out library books about great artists. They found material on people who were both artists and athletes. They made a conscious effort not only to praise Mark's art, but also to praise art itself as a desirable and important talent.

While living in Washington, D.C., we were invited to attend a concert given by the Yamaha School of Music at the Kennedy Center. Because we encountered difficulties in finding a babysitter, we came within a hair's breadth of not going, but we will be forever grateful that we did.

Two nine-year-olds, two eleven-year-olds, one fourteen-year-old, and one fifteen-year-old were to perform their own compositions. "How good can this be?" I wondered as I reflected on the skill-level of my own nine-year-old.

As the children were introduced, they looked just like children. The nine-year-old girls were dressed in lovely pastel dresses and lacy white anklets and Mary Jane shoes.

As the first nine-year-old took her seat at the piano, she carefully placed her hands in her lap and then held them above the keys, poised to begin. I was still not prepared for what I was to hear. After the first minute my mouth dropped open, and I don't think I closed it for the duration of the concert. Her own original composition seemed to me just short of miraculous. I couldn't believe that what I was hearing was not an adult virtuoso.

It went from miraculous to even better as the second nine-year-old took her place at a huge synthesized instrument similar to an organ with several keyboards, and a hundred or so stops and foot pedals. By intermission, when each child had performed an astounding original composition, I was heartsick that our children and my mother and everyone else I knew were not there to see and hear it.

After the intermission, three of the youngsters again performed original pieces, but this time with the Washington National Symphony under Rostropovitch, the great maestro and cellist. Again I could hardly believe what I was hearing.

Then, as though that were not enough, all the children were seated at the front of the stage for the last section. Volunteers from the audience were then each asked to play a two-measure theme on the piano. The children were to use those eight or ten notes as the basis of a three- to four-minute spontaneous composition, using proper chord structure, rhythm, and harmony. Volunteers did come forward and did play short, eight-note melodies previously unheard by the children. Each child, in turn, took the theme and turned it into a beautiful four- or five-minute rendition.

To ice the cake, before the last theme was presented, the request from the moderator was that the composition be a duet! The two nine-year-olds quickly volunteered, one on the piano, the other on the synthesized organ and their performance brought those in the audience to their feet shouting "Bravo! Bravo!"

Every person in that concert hall went home with a new appreciation of children and their talents. We went home more convinced than ever of the responsibility each person has to develop the gifts he is given.

Those children were obviously prodigies, yet I wished I could have studied their backgrounds. I suspect that they must have come from families who were keenly aware of their children's gifts and had searched for the best way to develop them. Because the children evidenced such serenity and enthusiasm, I'm sure the children felt that they had been given a special gift at a very early age, and they were determined to do something about it!

Though I realize that not many children are as gifted, I certainly left that auditorium understanding that my children's potential was much greater than I had given them credit for. I recommitted myself that night to look harder for the real gifts and talents of my children and to help them develop their own appreciation for those gifts along with a deeper feeling of responsibility for their development.

B. Methods

1. *Five-facet review.* (To assist parents in recognizing children's gifts and becoming aware enough of them to help their development.)

Do what Mr. and Mrs. Caine did. Set aside some time to think together about each child. Talk about their physical, mental, emotional, social, and spiritual capacities. Prompt each other's thinking. Ask each other what you have noticed about each of the five facets of each child. Take notes. Analyze.

Here's a promise: you'll *discover* things about your children—their character, their gifts, their potential—in this kind of a one-on-one brainstorming discussion that neither of you has ever thought of before.

Here's another promise: you'll enjoy it! And you will think of specific things to do that will be important in the development of your children's gifts.

Do it at least once a month.

2. *A simple nature walk.* (To help small children appreciate what God has given us and begin to feel responsible for those physical gifts.)

Few things are as exhilarating as taking a walk in the outdoors with a little child. The early spring or late autumn may be the best time, but any season is wonderful. He will show you more than you show him. If he doesn't point, follow his eyes.

Help him appreciate what he sees. Tell him in every way possible that Heavenly Father loves us so much that he made all of this for us.

Pick up litter as you go. Talk about how important it is to care for the earth. Talk about how good Heavenly Father feels when He sees His world being kept clean and beautiful as it was when He made it.

3. *Records.* (To help children appreciate their physical bodies and to see how use of them can improve how well they work.)

Set up a series of four or five physical events, such as a fifty-yard dash, a standing broad jump, or a tennis ball throw. Time or measure each child's performance in each event and record it in a family scrapbook or a bulletin board chart; explain that you'll do it again in a couple of weeks. Show the children how they can practice to improve their records. Be sure you emphasize that they are practicing to improve their own best, that they are competing only against themselves. Offer prizes to anyone who breaks his own record at the next "meet." Discuss how our bodies grow healthier as they are exercised and as muscles grow stronger.

4. *Toy stewardship.* (To help children understand the idea of having something being loaned to them, with the promise that if they take care of it, they may later have it for their own.)

Think of something that your child wants and that you have been planning to get him. Whatever it is, loan it to him rather than giving it. Say, "Johnny, this tennis racket is mine. I bought it with my money, and it belongs to me. I think you should have one, but I want to be sure you can take care of a tennis racket. I'm going to let you use this racket and take care of it for me. It will be just as though it's yours except that I'll take it back if you don't take care of it. You should always keep it in its place, always put the cover on it when you're not using it, and spray the strings each week so they won't get dry and break. If you take really good care of it, I will give it to you."

Then follow up. Remind him often. You want to give the

racket to him, so be sure he succeeds. After a couple of weeks, praise him extensively and give him the racket.

At the same time that you give it to him, explain to him that this is exactly the way that Heavenly Father deals with us. He has loaned us the beautiful earth, our bodies, our talents and gifts, and he has promised us that if we take good care of them, he will one day give them to us for our very own.

Then, while the idea is fresh, you may want to go directly into method 5 or 6. The stage will be set for children to understand.

5. *The Parable of the Talents.* (To help children see that it is important to develop the gifts and talents the Lord gives us.)

Depending on the ages of your children, you may want to read this Bible story directly from the scriptures (Matthew 25:14-30), or you may choose to tell it in your own words or read it from a Bible storybook. Explain that the master in the story is like our Heavenly Father. He wants us to develop and use the talents he has given us in order to make them grow. If we "bury" them by not using them, he takes them away. You can reinforce this principle by giving each child two pieces of paper. One child hides his paper. The others each tear theirs neatly in half so they end up with twice as many pieces. Then the master comes back and takes away the paper buried by the one child, tears it in half, and gives it to the children who multiplied their talents.

Children seven or older will understand this concept easily, but even a four-year-old can usually grasp the notion that Heavenly Father expects us to use the gifts He gives us, and that He is so pleased when we do this that He gives them to us forever and even adds other gifts to them. Immediately after the story, apply it personally to the children. Ask a child who sings well what will happen to her gift if she "buries" it and never uses it. Help her see that it will be taken away simply by never being developed.

Refer back to method 3. Help the children to see that their

bodies are like the talents. If they use them, they will grow and get stronger.

6. *Which is which?* (To help children understand that while man-made things wear out and get used up, God-given things do the opposite—they get stronger and multiply as we use them properly.)

Prepare a simple chart by drawing a line vertically down the center of a poster. Label one side "God-given—when we use them they get better or get stronger or multiply." Label the other side "Man-made—when we use them they wear out or are used up." (You might also use a flannelboard, a bulletin board, or even a table or the floor with a line of string separating the two labeled sides.)

Then, on prepared cards (or flannel-backed stick-ons, depending on how elaborate you want to be), show the children some items one at a time, and let them decide which side of the chart they should go on. For example, you may write on cards (one item to a card) these items: our arms, a toy truck, potatoes, a TV set, a lovely singing voice, a bag of candy, and so on.

As the children point to which side of the chart each items fits on, discuss why. Our arms get stronger as we use them and exercise them. A truck wears out. Potatoes, if you cut them up and plant them in the ground, grow lots more potatoes. A TV set wears out. When we sing and study music, our voices get better. A bag of candy gets used up.

Help the children to see, once again, that the God-given things really still belong to God, but that if we make them better as He wants us to, He'll let us keep them forever.

7. *Gratitude-related methods.* (To help children feel the kind of genuine gratitude to God that spawns feelings of indebtedness, obligation, and responsibility to him.)

(a) *Thankful thing.* Each Sunday ask a small child (preschooler) to draw something for which we should be particularly thankful to God during that week (the rain, that Billy recovered from the flu, that Grandma's operation went well). What he draws may not be recognizable, but it will symbolize the "thankful thing." Put it on the refrigerator or somewhere where it can be seen during family prayer and included in every prayer that week.

(b) *Gratitude list.* Gather the family and make a list, on large paper with a felt-tip marker, of the things God has given you. We like to do this rather formally, as a family tradition, on Thanksgiving day each year. This can also be an in-the-car game where people take turns naming blessings and continue to be part of the game as long as they can think of another thing each time it is their turn. In either case, frequent opportunities are created for emphasizing that we are responsible to take care of all that God has given us.

(c) *"Aren't we blessed!"* Anytime something good happens to you or to any member of your family, form a habit of saying, "Aren't we blessed!" Include things as great as a new baby and as small as a nice meal. Say it ten times a day, and use it as a way to focus children's attention on how much God has given them.

(d) *Prayer.* Prayer itself, the prayers your children hear you give, can be powerful teaching tools. As you thank God for His gifts, tell Him (as your children listen) that you are not only thankful, but you are also responsible. You want to care for all that He has given you because you want to keep it always. Ask Him to help you to do so. Encourage the children to ask for the same thing.

8. *Horizon-expanding methods.* (To help children realize that there are a great many interesting aspects to life and that they have the power to explore and to discover their own personal gifts and interests.)

(a) *Interesting things at dinner.* A good, around-the-table discussion at dinner time can be instigated by saying, "Let's all think quietly for a moment about the most interesting thing we saw or heard or had happen to us today. When you've thought of something, put your knife in front of your plate. When everyone has one, we'll go around the table and hear them all."

This can become a fascinating daily tradition. As it unfolds, it will give you opportunities to notice where your children's interests and abilities lie and to encourage their further development.

(b) *New experiences*. In connection with method *a* above, find ways to encourage your children to try new things to see if they are good at them or interested in them. Help them see that trying new experiences is the only way to find out how good we might be at them. Encourage them to volunteer for a service project, to try out for the school play, and so forth.

(c) *Early bedtime and reading*. Children as well as parents usually waste the golden hours between dinner and bedtime. Too much television is watched while too little constructive discussions or experiences or learning-oriented activities occur. One way to improve on this time is a bedtime policy where the children go to bed an hour before the time you think they should be asleep. If you can supply them with library books that will catch their interest and expand their vision, the hour can become a timely, valuable one. The most direct and effective way to do it is simply to set the hour-earlier bedtime and then tell the children that they can choose between going right to sleep and reading for an hour. Even nonreaders will choose to read when given such alternatives. This policy will work only if you are willing to exert the effort to help find genuinely interesting reading materials for each child. If you include your children in the library search, you will gain a bonus advantage—additional insight into their likes and dislikes.

C. Family Focal Points: Five-facet Review, Family Tree, Experts Board, Gift Abbreviations, Family Garden

We have found several of the foregoing methods fruitful and fun enough that we carry them on beyond the particular month that we are concentrating on "Responsibility for Gifts." The "early bedtime and reading" policy has become a pleasure for us all, as has the "interesting things at dinner" discussion period.

There are two or three even more basic practices that we would like to suggest to help you instill the responsibility for gifts in your children's minds, procedures you may find you are able to do on an ongoing basis without any great repeated commitment of time or energy.

Linda and I have a special date once each month, usually to a quiet restaurant that lends itself to thoughtful conversation. There we hold our "five-facet review" (method 1 from this chapter). We always come home with more insight into each child and with more specific ideas about how to help each.

We have a "family tree" on our wall with pictures of the children's grandparents, great-grandparents, and great-great-grandparents. From their respective journals we have extracted short stories about several of them that are both entertaining and illustrative of their personalities and gifts. We have looked for talents in these ancestors that are similar to some of the talents we see in our children. The children, in seeing those connections, are reinforced both in their appreciation of their gifts and in the responsibility for development that is implied.

On the wall of our playroom we also have a "family experts board," divided into thirty or forty small squares, each noting one particular gift of a certain child. For instance, "Saydi—good at singing harmony." "Talmadge—good at doing somersaults." The board is updated as children mature and as new gifts become evident.

A related practice came about one day quite by chance. I hold a brief, private interview each Sunday with each child, and one of my objectives is to build self-esteem by complimenting each one on his or her gifts. One Sunday six-year-old Josh, who soaks up praise and compliments like a sponge, got so excited as I was telling him what he is good at that he said, "Write those good things down, Dad, with your pen!"

"Where shall I write them, Josh?"

He looked around, smiled, and said, "On my hand!"

He wanted those good things where he could see them, where he could be reminded of how good he was. So I did; I wrote on one finger "math," on another "art," on another "fixing things." He didn't want to wash his hand!

The next week he wanted to do it again. We simplified it to a small abbreviation on the tip of each finger. By the following week, all of the children wanted the same thing, and it became a weekly tradition. I now use a pen with ink that washes off easily, and I'm still amazed at how those little visual symbols of individual gifts make children feel happier, more secure, and more inclined to be responsible to use and develop their talents.

One final method—a common and obvious one, but one that is very effective—is a family garden. We let each child be responsible for one separate crop. If they weed and water it, they get results; if they don't weed and water it, they don't reap the reward. The law of the harvest is obvious and graphic to them. We try to apply the lesson to all of God's gifts. If they are cared for responsively, they grow; if not, they don't.

Responsibility for the Holy Ghost... 9
from calmness to guidance

As a comforter, a verifier of truth, a guidance giver, the Holy Ghost is in many ways responsible for us. Ironically, the Holy Ghost cannot fulfill His responsibility until we become responsible for receiving Him and His gift.

A. Definition and Illustration

Are we responsible for the Holy Ghost? Or is He responsible for us? Most of us haven't thought much about those questions.

The Holy Ghost is a gift from God, in many ways the most useful and important of all His gifts. As with each of God's gifts, we are responsible for it. We are responsible to God to *receive* this great gift and to *retain* it. So are our children, even though they are so very young when it is given to them.

The Holy Ghost Himself is perfect in His own responsibility of giving us the guidance, comfort, and assistance we need, ask for, and are worthy of. Our responsibility, then, is simply to meet the conditions that make Him responsible for helping us.

James was an hour late getting home from school. He was only six, and his puffy eyes told his mother that there was a rather unpleasant reason for his lateness. They sat down together, and James explained:
"I walked home with Tommy because he said it was on my way. But after he went in his house I started walking and couldn't remember where my house was. I started going back to Tommy's but then I couldn't find his house either. All the houses looked kind of the same, so I started to cry. There was no one around to help me. Then I remembered I could talk to Heavenly Father. I shut my eyes and asked Him to help me. After a minute I felt better, and I saw Jenson's house at the end of the road, and I remembered that our road was the next one over."

James's puffy face was beaming. His mother held him close and told him of a similar experience she had had when she was a little girl. They talked about how the scared feeling went away when James prayed and how the calm feeling that came was the Holy Ghost.

A few weeks later, James watched a monster movie on television that he shouldn't have and began asking for the light left on in his room at night; the night light didn't satisfy him. After a week or so of nightly confrontations, his mother remembered what a strong impression James's earlier prayer—and its results—had made on him.

The next night she sat on the edge of his bed and said, "James, remember when you were lost and you prayed, and Heavenly Father sent the Holy Ghost to help you find your way home? Why don't you say another special prayer and ask for the Holy Ghost to help you not be afraid and so you feel calm."

James's face brightened up. They said a prayer together, a rather long and slow one. The feeling came, and James felt it. He learned something much more important than not being afraid of the dark.

The responsibility for the Holy Ghost is not only a great parental teaching obligation; it is also a great opportunity to place our children, as they mature, more and more in the care of this great spirit, and thus move more and more out of the realm of our care.

The Holy Ghost can do so much for those who accept the responsibility of receiving and retaining His presence. Both the receiving and the retaining take effort and real comprehension. The struggle is more than worth it. Consider Parley P. Pratt's description of the things the Spirit can do to one's personality and character:

"It inspires, develops, cultivates, and matures all the finetoned sympathies, joys, tastes, kindred feelings, and affections of our nature. It inspires virtue, kindness, goodness, tenderness, gentleness and charity. It develops beauty of person, form, and features. It tends to health, vigor, animation, and social feeling. It invigorates all the faculties of the physical and intellectual man. It strengthens, and gives tone to the nerves. In short, it is, as it were, marrow to the bone, joy to the heart, light to the eyes, music to the ears, and life to the whole being." (*Key to the Science of Theology* [Salt Lake City: Deseret Book Company, 1978], p. 61.)

As we attempt to bring this great force into our lives, we find that, in several ways, meeting this responsibility facilitates the meeting and teaching of all the other forms of responsibility. When children have the Holy Ghost with them, they become teachable, calm, and far more responsible, in general, than they are or can be without His presence.

I was a junior in college and in a bus on the way across the country to the Hill Cumorah Pageant when I finally realized that the Holy Ghost is a real person. Everyone on the bus was "on a mission" and on a very high spiritual plane. We were discussing the Holy Ghost when that fact struck me unexpectedly and startlingly, almost as though a bird had flown into my face. The Holy Ghost is a comforter, an entity who likes to be present when my feelings are in tune. One of the great challenges in life, I have discovered over the years, is to maintain the commitment I take upon myself in the sacrament each Sunday to always be worthy to have the Holy Ghost with me.

I have also discovered that it takes a conscious, ever-present desire and effort to maintain an atmosphere that the Holy Ghost can dwell in. The effort is especially difficult during trying moments, such as the fourth time I fish the baby out of the toilet, or the twelfth time somebody whines and cries and steps on my toe while I'm trying to fix dinner. But making that effort is a responsibility and a necessity!

I must decide every morning how I am going to react to the inevitable crises during the day. If I walk out of the bedroom in the morning without having a solid commitment to be the calm and peaceful "eye" of the hurricane, the Holy Ghost doesn't have much chance to exert His influence.

B. Methods

1. Approaches for helping small children understand who the Holy Ghost is and how He makes us feel.

(a) *Coming down from heaven.* (To give children the perspective of where they came from, how much God loves them, and how dependent they are on Him and on His power.)

Explain briefly to the children how we all lived in heaven with Heavenly Father and how He put us here on earth in families and told us to love one another. Then ask the children if they want to do a "play" about that. You need five characters (or whatever number of children you have). Select one "mother" and one "father," and assign the others to be their "children." Sit or stand the "children" on a couch and sit the "parents" on the floor. Point out that the parents are on the earth and the children are still with Heavenly Father. Have the "parents" talk about how much they would like a little baby. Have them say a little prayer to Heavenly Father asking Him to send a baby to them. Then you play the role of Heavenly Father and say to the children in "heaven" (on the couch): "That nice man and lady you see on earth want a baby very much. Which of you wants to go down?" They all raise their hands, and you choose one. They explain that Heavenly Father has a way of putting each spirit in a tiny little baby that is growing in mommy.

At this point one "child" goes to join the "parents" (gets off the couch) and is the family's new baby. The parents are very happy and love the baby very much. Soon they ask for another spirit to come to their home.

When you have walked them through it once, let them repeat the play a few times, taking different roles, talking with "Heavenly Father" before they "come to earth," and so forth.

When you are finished, reinforce the reality of what you've been role-playing. Tell them that it really happened that way in their own family, and tell them that Heavenly Father made this world for us and that He has a special helper called the Holy Ghost, whom he sends to make us feel good and to help us choose what is right.

(b) *Feeling something real.* (To help children understand that the Holy Ghost is real and that we can feel Him *inside*.)

Gather the children around a popcorn popper—any kind will do; a hot-air popper works well, because it is easy to watch.

Make a batch of popcorn. While doing so stress the senses. Call attention to *sight* of the popping corn, the *sound* of its explosions, the *smell*, the *touch* of the rough, warm kernels, and finally the *taste* of the kernels, first without salt, then with salt, and then with butter.

When all have had some popcorn, seat them in a circle in a new location and ask them about each of the senses they experienced. Ask: "What did you see?" "What did you smell? Taste? Touch? Hear?" Explain that these are their senses.

Then tell them that you are going to talk about something that we can't taste, touch, smell, see, or hear, but that is just as real as popcorn. It is something we can *feel!*

Have a short discussion about the air and how we need it in order to breathe. Breathe in and out several times, and have them do the same. Tell them that even though we can't see it, hear it, smell it, taste it, or touch it, it is always there.

Then say, "I have a special machine that you've all seen that makes air move so that you *can* feel it." Get out a blow-dryer, or borrow one. Turn it on and let them feel its warmth on their arm or face. Ask them, "How did it feel? Was it warm?"

Then say, "We're going to talk about something that you can feel, and it's very warm, but instead of being a warm feeling outside, it's a warm feeling inside. It's called the Holy Ghost."

(c) *Mary Ann and the Holy Ghost.* (A story to help children understand the Holy Ghost is to be loved and not feared.)

Four-year-old Mary Ann was worried. She was so worried that she could hardly think about anything else. Her big brother, Benjamin, planned to be baptized next week, and her Mommy and Daddy kept saying that he was going to get the Holy Ghost to be with him forever.

"I can hardly go to sleep at night without the hall light on," she thought. "I'll never be able to sleep at night again with a *ghost* in the house. How come everyone seems so excited about it?"

Even Julie, her six-year-old sister, seemed happy, and *she* had to have her night light on as well as have her teddy bear put in the closet every night with the doors closed, just in case he "turned alive" in the night. "Even *I* know that's silly," Mary Ann thought. "Teddy bears never come alive at night."

But now they were talking about a real ghost! As the baptism date came closer and closer, Mary Ann worried so much that the night before the baptism she just couldn't think about it any longer without crying. "What if the Holy Ghost hides under my bed?" she thought. "Or what if it scares me when I get up in the night to go to the bathroom?"

She kept trying to tell herself that He might be friendly, like Casper the Friendly Ghost, but she wasn't sure. She just couldn't hold the tears back any longer. Her mother heard her sniffling in her bed and hurried in to see what was wrong.

"Mary Ann, why are you crying?" she asked. Mary Ann sat up and threw her arms around her mother's neck.

"I'm so worried," she cried. "Everyone is talking about the Holy Ghost that Benjamin is going to get tomorrow, and I'm scared that he'll follow me around or hide under my bed!"

Mary Ann's mother smiled a big, happy smile, and Mary Ann thought she was even trying not to laugh right out loud. But her smile made Mary Ann feel better very quickly.

"Oh, honey!" she exclaimed. "I'm so sorry I didn't tell you before! The Holy Ghost is not like the make-believe ghosts on TV that scare people. He's someone very real, but He lives in your heart and whispers to your mind to tell you what is right and what is wrong. Then you can always make the right decisions. His answers are soft and quiet and sweet, and it always makes you feel happy to know He is there. You can feel Him sometimes, even though you're only three. You can feel Him when we hold hands and have family prayer, or when you know that Daddy and I love you. I can tell by the pretty smile on your face that you might even be feeling Him right now!"

Then an even bigger smile appeared on Mary Ann's face, and, with a big sigh of relief, she said, "I see. He's the one who tells me it's good to go to bed when you say I should, even when I don't want to, and He makes me feel happy when I share my toys."

"Right," said Mommy, squeezing Mary Ann's hand, "and even though its's very nice to feel that sometimes when you're little, tomorrow Benjamin will receive the *gift* of the Holy Ghost. That means that he can have Him in his heart all the time if he does what Heavenly Father says to do. Now go to sleep and think how excited Benjamin must be about having his new friend."

"Okay, Mommy," she said. As she snuggled down into the covers she thought, "I can hardly wait until *I'm* eight and I can have the gift of the Holy Ghost too!"

(d) *Which would you rather feel?* (To help children want to feel the calmness of the Holy Ghost's spirit.)

If you have a puppy or a docile dog, use it for this demonstration. If not, use the softest, warmest stuffed animal you can find.

Blindfold one or more of the children. Have them each feel the puppy or stuffed animal. Talk about how it feels (warm, soft, nice). Then have the children feel an ice cube. Talk about how it feels (cold, hard). Have them feel something rough and unpleasant, like sandpaper. Then take the blindfolds off and talk about the differences in how things feel.

Ask the children how they feel *inside* when their mother

or father gives them a big love (warm, happy). Tell them that that is how Heavenly Father's spirit feels—calm, warm, soft, nice. And when we are kind to each other, His spirit likes to be there, so we feel warm and happy inside.

(e) *Three things that rhyme and that bring the Spirit.* (To help children understand the connection between doing right and feeling good.)

Set up a chalkboard or use a large sheet of paper. Give three small sheets of paper to each child.

Tell the children that they are going to learn to read three important words, and that the three words all rhyme. Tell them that the amazing thing about the three words is that they each help us to have the Holy Ghost with us.

On the large paper or chalkboard write, vertically, *1, 2, 3*. Next to *1*, write PRAYER. Tell the children what it says, and have each of them draw a small picture of a child praying. (It doesn't matter if what they draw is not recognizable.) Then talk about prayer and about the four steps of prayer: open in Heavenly Father's name, say thank you to Him, ask Him for good things, and close in Jesus' name and with *Amen*.

Talk about why we kneel for prayer. Then kneel in a circle and say a simple prayer while they fold their arms. Let some of them pray, too. It may help, prior to the prayer, to discuss what you are thankful for and what things you should ask for.

At a particularly calm moment after a prayer, ask the children how they feel—like the puppy or teddy bear, or like the ice cube or sandpaper? Do they feel warm and safe? Who makes us feel that way? (Holy Ghost.) Is He here? (Yes.) Why? What brought Him here? (The prayer.)

Reinforce the idea that *prayer is just one way to bring the spirit* or the warm feeling. Then say, "What else can bring the Holy Ghost here besides prayer?" By the number *2*, write SHARE. Have the children look at the word and say it for several moments. Explain the word. Have them say *prayer* and *share*. Point out that they sound the same, or rhyme.

Do some short role-playing on sharing (for example, two

children who want the same toy yell and fight over it). Then have them start over, but this time they will take turns. When do they feel happy and warm? When do they feel mad and sad?

Ask: What made us feel warm and happy? (The Holy Ghost.) What brought him here? (When we shared.)

Tell the children that we now know two sure ways to get the Holy Ghost to come, and they rhyme. Can you read them? *Prayer* and *share*.

Have each child draw a picture of two children sharing. Then say, "There is another sure way to get the Holy Ghost to come, and it rhymes too." Write CARE by the number 3, on the paper or board.

Explain that when someone needs help, there are two things we can do: one is to care and help them; the other is to *not* care and not help them.

Make two signs on small pieces of paper. One says, *Care*, the other says *care* with a line through it to cross it out. Pin the signs on two of the children. Then role-play several simple situations in which a third child pretends to need help (can't take his coat off, lost his nickel, can't put a lid back on something). The child wearing the sign with the word *care* crossed out walks past the one needing help. The one with the care sign stops and helps. Then ask, "Which one made you smile and feel good?" (The "care" one.) What does *care* mean? (To help.) Why do we feel good when we care? (Because the Holy Ghost comes.)

Have the children draw a picture of someone who is caring.

Review again who the Holy Ghost is and how He makes us feel. Then go back to the list of three words and point at them over and over until the children can read them in unison. Then ask, "How can we get the Holy Ghost to come?"

Reemphasize that there are three main ways, that they all rhyme, and that they all work: *prayer*, *share*, *care*.

Hang the sign with the three words on the wall and refer

to it often. "Can you remember the words? What happens when we do them?" (The Holy Ghost comes.)

2. *Programming yourself to be calm.* (To help you, as a parent, to radiate the kind of contagious calm that rubs off so effectively onto your children.)

Children are exceptionally accurate mirrors. When we are frustrated or nervous and anxious for any reason, our children will, quite predictably, follow suit and become either stubborn, whiny, obstinate, or irritable, or a combination of these attitudes. It does little good to teach them that they are responsible for how they act unless we set the proper example.

Our common mistakes are: (1) to bring outside frustrations into the home and let them affect our children; and (2) to react thoughtlessly to a child's misbehavior in a way that sets no better example for him than he is setting for us.

As Linda mentioned earlier in this chapter, both mistakes can be corrected by programming yourself to be calm and peaceful. The process is simple. Find a particular moment, a certain time each day when you can decide in advance to react with control and calm to whatever family situations arise. For most mothers, the best time is early, before the fast pace of the day takes over. Set aside five minutes alone, perhaps in the bath or shower or just in your room before you emerge to face the day. Let the day's schedule pass through your mind. Think of the little irritations that are likely to arise: the spilled milk, two children demanding attention at the same time, the fighting over a toy—you'll know what they are from experience. Make up your mind to react calmly when they occur. *Decide in advance.* We usually don't decide how we'll react until we are *in* a situation. The key to avoiding a less than calm response, which drives away the Holy Ghost's presence, is to decide how we will react before the situation occurs.

Fathers can do the same thing. An early morning jog or run is probably the best time and place of all to self-program for either father or mother. Fathers can also find a moment of self-programming beneficial when it is used to make the mental transition from work to home. Before you leave the car, dismiss the frustrations and concerns and mind-occupying carryovers from the job, and shift mental gears. Make yourself conscious of your family. Think through the stressful situations that may await you inside the front door. The house may be a mess. Dinner may not be ready. There may be some problem with the children. Think through the possibilities and decide in advance to react to all of them with calmness and understanding in order to attract the Holy Ghost's presence.*

3. *The "Still Small Voice."* (A song about the Holy Ghost and His calming influence, which helps children to understand and want His presence.)

Sing this song (B-92 in *Sing with Me*) occasionally as a family and discuss the words. It is a good attention-getter and sets the stage to review some of the ways we can invite the Holy Ghost to be with us.

4. *Methods involving prayer.* (To help children realize that the most beautiful and predictable way to obtain the Holy Ghost's presence is the practice of sincere prayer.)

(a) *We have to open the door.* If possible, obtain a copy of the painting that shows Christ standing at the door with a light, but there is no doorknob or latch on His side of the door. *We* have to open the door. Explain to the children that the door is opened through prayer. If the picture is unobtainable, you might draw one, or have a child draw his version of the intended idea.

(b) *Answering a prayer.* (For very young children.) Pretend that your voice is Heavenly Father's as He listens and responds to your child's prayer. Don't use this idea unless you explain it *very* carefully to your children. Make sure they

---

*For a more detailed treatment of self-programming for fathers, see Richard M. Eyre, *Simplified Husbandship, Simplified Fathership* (Salt Lake City: Bookcraft, 1980).

know that you are only saying what Heavenly Father *might* be thinking as He listens to their prayers. As a child prays, respond warmly and lovingly. For example:

"Heavenly Father."

"Yes, Johnny, I'm pleased that you are talking to me tonight."

"I thank thee for this nice day."

"You are welcome. I'm glad you enjoy the blue sky that I made."

"And I thank thee for my mommy and daddy."

"You're welcome. They are wonderful parents, and they love you very much."

"Bless me that I will have a good day at school tomorrow."

"I will, Johnny, and you remember to set a good example while you're there."

"Please send the Holy Ghost to help me and guide me."

"I'm glad you asked for the Holy Ghost, Johnny. He is my helper, and I will send Him. He will make you feel calm and strong and will help you to choose the right."

Reemphasize that prayer itself is very real and that you were only pretending to be Heavenly Father's voice. But He does listen, and He will send the Holy Ghost to help us if we ask.

(c) *Code word for super powers.* Play the following game with your children:

"Let's pretend that there is someone named Hogo who has super powers, who lives on a faraway planet, and who will come and help us whenever we say the secret code. Now, the secret code is 'A-B-C.' Have you got it?

"Now let's pretend that Wally [substitute your child's name] is really worried about a test at school tomorrow. He has studied hard, but he feels nervous and uneasy inside, and he's afraid he'll forget everything he's learned." (Wally says "A-B-C" and Hogo, represented by Dad or Mom or another child, comes down and whispers the test answers to Wally so he can remember them on the test.)

"Now, Susan [substitute the name of one of your children], let's pretend something really sad. Let's pretend that your dog got run over by a car, and you felt so bad that you just didn't think you would *ever* stop crying." (Susan says "A-B-C," and Hogo comes down and puts his arm around her and tells her that her dog's spirit is all right and that she'll feel better soon.)

"Now, Wally, your turn again. Pretend that you are trying really hard to decide whether you should take piano lessons. Your mother wants you to, and you yourself want to, but you don't know if you can do it well, so you are wondering if you should try or not." (Wally says "A-B-C," and Hogo comes down and says he'll help Wally to learn. He puts Wally's hands on the keys and pushes down the right fingers to play a little song. He tells Wally to go ahead and not to worry because he'll be there to help whenever Wally says "A-B-C."

Then say to the children, "Would you like to really be able to say 'A-B-C' and have Hogo come down to help you whenever you needed him?" Explain that there really is someone with super powers who can help us but he is invisible, and his name isn't Hogo—it's *the Holy Ghost.* And the code word really isn't "A-B-C"—it's *prayer.*

5. *Discussion on foreordination and decisions.* (To help children who have been baptized to realize that they have been foreordained to do certain things and that the Holy Ghost will guide them in decisions regarding that foreordination.)

Use the following questions to generate a discussion:

(a) Where did we live before this life? (with Heavenly Father)

(b) Why did He send us here? (so we could have families and be happy and learn how to be our best selves)

(c) What did He give to each of us before we left? (a special blessing that told us certain things we should do while we're down here)

(d) Can you remember what those things in the blessing were? (no)

(e) Then how can you be sure you do them? (I don't know. How?)

(f) Who *does* know what those things are? (Heavenly Father)

(g) Does His helper, the Holy Ghost, know? (yes)

(h) Will He help us to find what they are and to do them? (yes)

(i) What do we have to do to get that help? (Pray for it)

(j) When you need to make a decision, such as whether or not to smoke a cigarette, will He help you? (yes) Is that an easy one? (yes)

(k) When you need to make a more complicated decision, such as what classes to take in school, will He help you then too? (yes)

(l) How? (by giving me a good feeling about the classes I should take)

(m) Do we have to *ask* Heavenly Father when we want the Holy Ghost's help? (yes)

C. Family Focal Points: Morning Quiet Time, Dinner-hour Calm, Sunday Traditions, Priesthood Use

While there are many appropriate and wonderful ways to help children accept their responsibility for retaining the Holy Ghost after that gift has been given, we focus most of our ongoing efforts into three distinct time slots: early morning, dinner time, and Sundays.

1. Early morning. The way in which a day is started often has an influence on the mood and feeling of the entire day. In the Eyre family, we find that if we can begin our days with a calm, quiet, loving feeling, the battle is more than half won. Our older children practice violin and piano before breakfast and school. Our pattern and tradition is that everyone must speak very softly as he gets up and goes about his practicing. When someone speaks loudly or crossly, a finger to the lips is our signal to remember that it is quiet time. When it is time for breakfast, we kneel around the table, and whoever prays includes a word of thanks for the sweet, calm spirit of the Holy Ghost that we have felt already that morning, and a request that we may have that spirit with us during the rest of the day.

2. *Dinner time.* We insist that dinner time also be a time of peace and calm. It is fine for children to be excited about school, or about the ballgame that night, or whatever, but they must express this enthusiasm quietly and must talk in turn.

We have a big brass bell that summons the family to dinner. We have tried to arrange the dinner hour so that everyone can be there, and the children know that they must be kneeling at their chairs within sixty seconds of the bell's ring. After the prayer, all are asked to think for a moment of the most interesting thing they saw, heard, or had happen to them during the day. (See chapter 8.) The discussion is a peaceful one, and the rule is that anyone who disturbs that spirit receives warning and then, on a second violation, has to go to his room until he is ready to behave calmly and peacefully.

3. *Sundays.* We believe that Sundays are the key not only to teaching this responsibility but to the strength and spirit of the family institution. We make it a point to do at least four things as a family each Sunday: (a) Have the Sunday session goal-setting period (see chapter 12) and interviews (see chapter 8). (b) Read one or two ancestor stories (see chapter 6). (c) In preparation for the sacrament, we show a portion of the film *Jesus of Nazareth* on videotape to help smaller children visualize Jesus and be better able to think about Him when they partake of the sacrament. We show a different portion of His life each week so that the little ones can visualize Him in a new way each time. The older children read with us from the book *What Manner of Man* (Richard M. Eyre, [Salt Lake City: Bookcraft], 1979), which portrays a different, separate facet of the Lord's personality and char-

acter for each week of the year. We also bring a small book we have assembled featuring pictures of the Savior that we particularly like for the small children to look at during the sacrament. They know from the time they are very small that the purpose of the sacrament is to remember Jesus and what He did for us. As they pass the age of eight, of course, they know it is also a time to remember the promises they made at their own baptisms. (d) We decide as a family on one "secret service" that we will perform during the coming week, some act of service or kindness that we can do anonymously.

Each of these four practices seems to have a calming, unifying influence on our family. They also offer many opportunities to reinforce with the children how having the gift of the Holy Ghost is a privilege as well as a responsibility, and that now that they have been given this gift, they are responsible to God to use it, to live by it, and to find out what the Lord wants them to know through it.

One other learning experience is a further key to having the Lord's Spirit in the home:

We once attended a fireside of Harvard graduate students and their wives, and the speaker was a wonderful General Authority who, rather than speak, let us ask him questions. One young father, a close friend of ours, asked, "How can we have the Holy Ghost more consistently and continuously in our homes?" I expected a long answer, several points, or a formula. Instead the answer was four words: "Use the priesthood more!" We all looked a little puzzled, so the speaker went on: "Priesthood power is intended to be used in our families, for it draws the Holy Ghost's presence. Most of us don't use this power often enough. We reserve it for life-and-death situations and otherwise let it atrophy and lie dormant. I think that a little girl afraid of a big test in school is important enough for a priesthood blessing. I think that a child with a fever and unable to sleep is important enough for a priesthood blessing, or a wife who has had a particularly hard day, or a son who is facing a big decision. If you want the Spirit to dwell more in your home, use the priesthood more."

In our home each of the children receives a blessing on his or her birthday concerning the year ahead. Their mother keeps notes on the blessings that go into their journals. I also bless the family if I am going to be away on business for two consecutive nights or more. Priesthood blessings are given upon request by children who understand God's power and see specific applications for that power.

Additionally, we have dedicated our homes by the power of the priesthood and blessed them as peaceful and safe havens for the love and mutual respect of our family.

SECTION III

RESPONSIBILITY TO SELF (DISCIPLINE)

A study at a major university attempted to delineate the factors involved in the typical human's ability to translate the acceptance of an idea into the implementation or application of that idea, to motivate us to turn thought into action. The results were as follows:

Step	Probability of Implementation
1. Hear an idea that you like	10%
2. Consciously decide to adopt the idea	25%
3. Decide when you will do it	40%
4. Plan how you will do it	50%
5. Commit to someone else that you will do it	65%
6. Have a specific future appointment with the person you committed to, at which time you will report to him whether you have done it	95%

Basically, what the study shows is that most people don't have enough self-discipline and self-motivation to accomplish the things they've committed themselves to. They are too dependent on supervision or the follow-through of others.

When children feel responsible to someone else, to their parents, or to God, factors 5 and 6 come in as strong motivations. When the main responsibility for accomplishment is to themselves, they need an inner form of motivation. They need to develop the self-discipline that drives them forward even when no one else is watching or checking up. They need to have self-respect in order to implement the first four steps on the chart; then they need to commit to themselves in a way that is as motivational as committing to someone else.

To be obedient requires one level of maturity. To accept stewardship requires a higher level of maturity. And to be self-disciplined requires a still higher level of maturity.

In the crucial and pivotal years after

the children have been baptized—as they complete their last years of elementary school, as the boys prepare to receive the priesthood, and as the girls begin the first steps of transition into womanhood—they need to become responsible to themselves, to develop firm self-discipline to control their directions and destinies.

This form of responsibility (responsibility to self) should not be viewed as a substitute or replacement for the earlier forms (responsibility to parents and to God) but rather as an addition to them, as a new dimension of responsibility that is more self-motivated than the other two, and that therefore increases a child's self-control and his ability to be responsible to others as well.

We never outgrow our responsibility to parents, and certainly not our responsibility to God. They are both deepened and enhanced when we add to them the inner strength of self-discipline. When a child gains a strong self-identity, he realizes that it is up to him what his life will be, and he begins to feel responsible to himself.

The awakening of those feelings—the inner motivations and strengths of self-discipline—is what this section is about.

Just as a person must learn to both love and fear God in order to feel fully responsible to Him, he must also both love and fear himself if he is to become truly self-disciplined. Out of love for himself—self-esteem—he will then take positive pride in his choices, his character, and his potential. Out of a healthy fear for his inconsistencies and "of-the-flesh" weaknesses, he will avoid the temptations and negative paths that produce weak choices, shallow character, and missed potential.

Responsibility for Choices ... from friendship to leadership

10

"If we could only make decisions for them!" we say. But we can't. In the long perspective all we can do—and it is a great deal—is to teach them how to decide for themselves.

A. Definition and Illustration

One of the ironies of life is that the most important and crucial decisions are thrust at us long before we have the wisdom to make them. Before we are a third of the way through life, we usually have to make some of the most far-reaching decisions of our entire lives—mission, marriage, field of study, occupation, location—along with the even more important ongoing decisions of values, morality, lifestyle, and priorities.

By the time children are ten or eleven years old, sometimes even earlier, factors important to these later decisions become evident. Those whom they choose for friends, what they decide to experiment with, which activities they devote interest and time to, whom they look up to and idolize, what they decide about their own status as leader or follower—these and many other choices begin to materialize and to shape the even larger decisions soon to come.

Children who can recognize the connections between what they decide now and what they will *be* later on, who begin to feel responsible for their own decisions, will greatly increase their chances to make mature and far-sighted decisions that create a foundation for a happy life. Such is the objective of the ideas and methods in this chapter.

Mario was a delightful child. People had been saying so since his birth ten years ago. He had a sunny personality that always fit in. He was well-liked by both adults and his peers. He was always part of the group, always "in" on everything. He was a serious-minded boy who had real faith, both in his parents and in God.

Then a year or so ago his parents began to see a potentially negative side to Mario's universal acceptance by others.

They began to realize that one of the main reasons he was always with the crowd was because he always went along with the crowd. Recently a group of boys had tortured a cat, swinging it by its tail, throwing it in water, pulling its ears, even tying a firecracker to its tail and injuring it seriously. Mario, whose sensitive and compassionate nature must have been repulsed by all this, went along with it anyway, presumably to preserve his place as part of the group. He had made other similar bad choices for similar reasons.

His parents, Manuel and Maria, knew that somehow they had to change the pattern. After some serious and prayerful thought, Manuel and Maria arranged to take Mario—just Mario—to a nice restaurant for a special dinner. Their topic of discussion was decisions.

They started by telling Mario that there are two kinds of decisions. One kind should be easy because Heavenly Father has already told us the right answers, and they apply to everyone. The second kind involves lots of options, and different ones are right for different people. Heavenly Father will help us with these too, but He has to tell us the answers personally, through our own prayers, when we face the decision and know what our options are.

Mario seemed to understand the distinction. They discussed examples of the first kind: whether we should go to church, whether we should pay tithing, whether we should be kind, whether we should hurt people (or animals), whether boys should go on missions. They discussed examples of the second kind: what classes to take in school, which activities to get involved in, whom to marry, what job to have, where to live.

Then his parents asked Mario when he thought was the best time to make each kind of decision. After some discussion, they arrived at the right answer together. Decisions of the first kind should be made now, in advance, because we already know the right answers and we shouldn't wait until we are in difficult situations before we commit ourselves to what's right. Decisions of the second kind must wait until we actually face them, and then we try to decide prayerfully and correctly.

They talked about examples and situations. "Let's say, Mario, that in a couple of years you are with your buddies, and they decide it would be fun to sniff some glue or to try some drugs. They are all doing it and saying how good it makes them feel, and they urge you to try it. When you hesitate they say, 'Come on, Mario, don't be chicken. It won't hurt you—no one will know.' If you haven't made your decision in advance, that might be a tough situation, but if you've already decided never to use drugs, it would be much easier, wouldn't it?"

The dinner meeting went on much longer than anyone had planned. But it was wonderful. Because he was treated like an adult, Mario responded like one. He enjoyed receiving so much attention from both parents, and his attention span seemed longer than they had remembered it.

The result of the discussion was a list, written in Mario's own hand, of all the decisions he was prepared to make right now, the things he could commit to himself and to his parents because he knew they were right. The list included keeping the Word of Wisdom and never using drugs, paying a full tithing, never doing anything cruel to a person or an animal, telling the truth no matter what, going on a mission, and never cheating.

As each item was added to Mario's list, he and his parents discussed situations in which holding to the decision would be difficult and temptation would be great. Mario recommitted himself in light of each of these imagined situations. When the list was finished, he dated and signed it. He put it in the front of his journal where he would see it often and would remember that those decisions were already made.

Before they left the restaurant, they also talked about the second kind of decisions. Manuel and Maria told Mario of times in their lives when they had important decisions to make and how they had prayerfully made those decisions and then taken them to Heavenly Father in prayer. They told of the warm feelings that had confirmed to them that their decisions were right and that they should go ahead. They talked about decisions Mario would have to make, and Mario began to understand the process by which confirmation can be gained for all such decisions.

When the evening was over, the foundation was laid, the trust level built, and the communication channels opened to permit future discussions about individual decisions that would arise. More importantly, Mario came away stronger, more aware of his responsibility to himself and of his control over his own destiny.

B. Methods

1. *Approaches to help small children define "decisions."* (To make the terms *choice* and *decisions* familiar to young children so the words and concepts can be used in later methods.)

(a) *Questions and discussion.* Ask:

What is a decision? What does it mean to make a decision? (When you choose or decide for yourself which thing you want or what you want to do.)

Have you made any decisions lately? Stimulate children's thinking by asking, Did you choose what to wear today? Did you choose where to sit on the sofa? Did you decide which book to look at when you first came to school? Did you decide whether to watch TV last night or to play with your toys? Did you decide to sleep with your teddy bear last night, or to have the door opened or closed?

Do you like to make decisions?

Do you ever make a wrong decision and wish you could change it? (Everyone does at one time or another. Sometimes we can change a decision and sometimes we can't. When we have a very important decision to make, we should think about it first and try to make a good decision that will make us happy.)

(b) *Puppet shows*. (To help children better understand what decisions are and to aid them in differentiating between decisions governed by laws or rules and decisions that have to be individually pondered and made.)

Using hand puppets, and a little imagination, do short puppet shows. Use the suggestions listed below or make up some of your own. The characters for the suggested skits are a mother, a father, two girls, and two boys. Any hand puppets will do as long as you identify who is who before each skit.

For a puppet stage, use the back of the sofa or large chair. Kneel behind it or behind a blanket stretched between the backs of two kitchen chairs. The children will be able to see your face, but tell them to pretend that they can't see you. (You should be able to watch them so that you can respond to their reactions.) You will talk for all the characters (one on each hand) and also make necessary explanations as you go along. The puppet who is speaking should be moving while the other one is still, so that the children may follow the story with ease.

Don't worry about your dramatic ability. No matter how amateurish the show is, the children will probably love it and will give their rapt attention. There should be two parts to each show. The first part should involve an unhappy ending, when the "puppet child" disobeys a rule or makes a bad decision. Then the same situation is repeated with a happy ending as the child obeys the rule or makes a good decision. Each show should be very short. You can dramatize three or four situations (with both endings) in about ten minutes. Discuss the decisions after each show.

Puppet Show 1

Characters needed: Three puppets—a mother and two girls.
The situation: A girl wants to wear her new dress instead of her long pants to school, though the weather is very cold. She discovers that her long tights, which she usually wears with a dress, are in the laundry.

First ending: She decides to wear the dress anyway, without her long tights. She is happy when her best friend compliments her on her pretty dress, but when they go outside to play, her legs are so cold that she must return to the building and cannot play with the other children. She realizes that she has made a bad decision.

Second ending: She decides to wear her long pants and to save the dress to wear on a warmer day. When the children go out to play, she is able to go with them. She realizes that she has made a good decision.

Puppet Show 2

Characters needed: Two puppets—a girl and a mother.

The situation: A girl finds a book of matches on the sidewalk. She knows the rule that she must never play with matches.

First ending: She decides to strike one of the matches. She is delighted that it works, and she becomes so interested in watching it burn that she doesn't blow it out in time, and her fingers are burned. She runs home to her mother, who treats the burns and comforts her. Her mother is disappointed that she broke the rule, but she doesn't punish the little girl; she explains that the girl has already been punished by being burned.

Second ending: The girl decides to take the matches home to her mother. Her mother praises her for obeying the rule.

Puppet Show 3

Characters needed: Three puppets—a mother, a father, and a boy.

The situation: A boy is told that his father is coming home from work early to take him to the circus. His mother says that he must clean his room up before he can go.

First ending: He decides to watch just one more cartoon on television before cleaning his room, but he gets interested in the TV and forgets about it. When his father comes home, the boy's room isn't cleaned up, and by the time the boy finishes the job, they arrive at the circus late and miss the first act. He realizes he has made a bad decision to watch TV first and then do his chores.

Second ending: He cleans his room up and then watches TV. He realizes he has made a good decision, for he is ready to go to the circus when his father arrives to take him.

Puppet Show 4

Characters needed: Three puppets—two boys and a father.

The situation: A little boy is walking home from school with a friend who asks him to come to his house to play for a while. He knows there is a family rule that he should go straight home from school and ask his parents for permission to go to a friend's home. His friend says, "You can call your mother on our phone."

First ending: He goes to his friend's home to call his parents, but the line is busy. Then he becomes interested in his friend's new game and forgets about calling home. About an hour later he suddenly remembers. He knows that he has broken a family rule, and so he hurries home. His parents are very upset and tell him that they have been very worried about him. They love him very much, but they must discipline him to help him remember to obey the rule. He is not allowed to have his friend over to his house, or to go to his friend's house, for a week.

Second ending: The little boy says, "I'll go home first and ask my parents if I can come to your house. Then, if I can, I'll be right back." His parents give him permission and praise him for remembering and obeying the rule.

2. *Righteous decision reinforcement.* (Ways to give *enough* praise and reinforcement for good decisions to *over-balance* the rebuttal and ridicule that may come from the "crowd" who wants your child to make the wrong decision.)

(a) *Ancestor stories.* Locate true stories about your own ancestors who had the courage to go against the crowd, to do what they believed was right, such as converting to the Church and leaving their homelands. Tell the experiences in a way that truly honors that courage and shows how much it pays off in the long run. Relate each ancestor to the child, such as telling him, "You are this man's great-grandson; the same kind of courage to do right that was in him is in you too."

(b) *Individual attention reinforcement.* In your "Sunday sessions" with your children (see chapters 8 and 12), spend some time talking about good choices they have already made. If they have prepared a list of decisions made in advance as suggested in the illustration at the beginning of this chapter, go through that list with them individually on a regular basis. Ask whether the anticipated situations have come up, and praise every incident where they adhered to their in-advance decision.

(c) *Prayer.* Encourage children, by example and advice,

to ask for help in holding firm on the decisions they have already made and in gaining guidance on the new choices that arise. Encourage them to thank Heavenly Father for His help during the specific times they have made correct decisions and been strong enough not to back down from decisions already made.

Occasionally, in your own prayers and while the children are listening, thank God for children who know how to choose the right and then stick to it. Thank Him for any individual instances you can think of wherein they did hold firm and choose right.

3. *Allowing natural consequences.* (The "innoculation principle"—to help children understand the cause-and-effect nature of their choices while they are *young*, before the decisions are weighty and the consequences serious enough to have adverse effects on their lives.)

The medical principle of innoculation operates on the premise that a small number of germs can threaten the body just enough to stimulate the production of antibodies. Likewise, small, relatively unimportant bad choices, with their attendant consequences, go further in teaching children to make good decisions than any amount of counsel, advice, or artificial punishment.

Examples of poor choices and possible consequences might include the following:

Failure to practice piano piece—embarrassment at the recital.

Wearing heavy clothing on a hot day—discomfort and irritation.

Watching late TV show on Friday—missing family outing early Saturday morning.

Failure to study for spelling test—low or failing grade.

There will be many situations in which you will have a clear choice between pushing your child to make the correct choice and letting him choose wrongly and suffer the consequences. The key is to be wise enough to let relatively unimportant choices, especially the ones with rather immediate and noticeable consequences, take their natural course.

When you do allow him wrong choices, be sure to discuss what happened and why it happened while it is still fresh in the child's mind. Always go from the specifics of what has just happened to the general principle that wrong decisions always catch up with us, whereas good choices always end up making us happy.

4. *Approaches relating to choice of friends.* (Hardly any subject concerns or occupies conscientious parents so much as their children's choice of associates and friends. It is sometimes easy to overreact, at other times easy to underreact. What is needed is a careful mixture of the two approaches that follow.)

(a) *Engineering good friendships.* If you are aware of a particular child who has some qualities that you feel would be good for your child to acquire, don't be afraid to "engineer" a little matchmaking. Most children under ten or eleven will become friends almost as a matter of course once they are brought together for a period of time. Call the child's parents and compliment them on the qualities you like in their child; they'll appreciate your comments. Then invite their child over for an afternoon, or take him on an outing with your family, or whatever. By bringing the children together in a relaxed atmosphere a couple of times, chances are a friendship will start.

(b) *Building up instead of tearing down.* Too often, when one of our children associates with another child whom we consider to be a negative influence, our first and only thought is to break the friendship up, to separate our child from the source of negative influence. In some cases this may be the appropriate—perhaps the only—thing to do. At other times, however, with a little thought, we could create a situation where our child helps or influences the other child to change.

Sometimes the process is simple. You may want to initiate a conversation such as the following: "Son, you know, Mike seems like a nice boy, but I was wondering if he does anything that he shouldn't, anything that you wouldn't do."

"Yes, he swears a lot."
"That's too bad. I wonder why he does that."
"I think his dad and mom do."
"Well, you two are pretty good friends, aren't you?"
"Yes."
"Do you think that if he's around you a lot and never hears you swear, he might not do it so much himself?"
"Maybe."
"I think he might not. You might even tell him that you think he should try not to swear. Tell him you like him a lot, but that he doesn't sound good when he swears."

The idea, of course, is to help your child develop leadership qualities and an ability that makes him more likely to influence and change others for good than to yield to a negative influence.

The major problems children have in elementary school often concern friends, not academics. And they are problems that, if not resolved, can affect their self-image into adulthood.

When children are small, their tastes are very indiscriminating. As they grow older, they begin to "weed out" a little. Often the girls eliminate boys from their list of friends, and vice versa. Friends who have similar interests become important, and children begin to appreciate what a real friend is.

Parents are inclined to feel that friends at this age are not terribly important. But friends are important for everyone, regardless of our age.

Because each child is so different, and no blanket statement can apply in all cases, we must teach children the principles of making friends. We should talk about it and give them some guidance. Too many children are left alone to sort these things out for themselves. If they are having problems with friends at school, they are usually reluctant to talk about it. Their frustrations often manifest themselves in anger and letting off steam at home for seemingly inexplicable reasons.

We can't emphasize strongly enough the need to talk to

children about their friends and to teach them how to make friends and how to influence them for good. Children are capable of understanding that making friends is an art.

5. *The brother of Jared.* (To help teach children that one of life's purposes is to teach us to make our own correct decisions, but that we can always check with the Lord to make sure they are right before we act upon them.)

Read to or tell your children the story of the brother of Jared in Ether 2:16 through 3:6. Emphasize that the first time Jared went to the Lord, he merely stated the problem: it's dark in the boats. The second time, he went with a solution for the Lord to confirm: I have mined these clear stones, and they will glow if you touch them.

Explain that if we make prayerful, careful decisions and take them to Heavenly Father in prayer, he will either confirm them through a calm and sure feeling that will help us know they are right, or He will give us a confused feeling that tells us to think through the whole decision once again.

You may want to tell of a personal experience or story that centers around the confirmation of the Holy Ghost when right decisions are made.

C. Family Focal Points: Advance Decisions, Family Council Decisions, "Leader for the Right"

While we were presiding over the London England Mission, one of our chief concerns centered on the critical decisions that would crowd in on the missionaries when they returned home. One of the easiest parts of a mission is that most of the decisions missionaries make involve simple questions of obedience. In terms of personal behavior, time priorities, and so on, mission rules and regulations cover most of their decisions. In this sense a mission is a respite from the dilemmas of personal choice-making. Yet when they return home, they are faced with the most crucial decisions of their lives. We wanted very much to send the missionaries home with the concepts and mental tools necessary to choose the right mate, the right field of work, the right life.

We did two things: (1) we held a seminar on how the missionaries could gain spiritual confirmation for their key decisions before implementing them; and (2) we asked them to spend time on their flight home preparing a careful list of the decisions they were prepared to make now, in advance, and to send us a copy.

Since then, we have decided that we need to follow the same procedure with our own children. Not long after they are baptized, usually when they are nine or ten, we work with them on a list of advance decisions. Like Manuel and Maria in the earlier illustration in this chapter, we ask them to imagine the hardest conceivable situation and then help them commit to standing by their decision. The lists go into their journals and are open-ended so that other advance decisions may be added as the need for them arises.

Parents usually have their own list of advance decisions that can be used as examples. We also have a list of family advance decisions that we have made together—decisions we have decided upon unanimously and absolutely. Some of them are: (1) that we will always accept the church callings that come to us; (2) that we will always be totally honest with each other; (3) that we will always support one another's interests and activities; and (4) that we will always pray for one another.

When major family decisions must be made that fall outside of our advance-decision list, we make them together, in a family council, following the same procedure we hope the children will learn to follow in their individual decisions. First, we pray for God's guidance in our thinking. Second, we analyze and discuss every aspect, every pro and con, every consequence we can think of. Third, we come to our own best decision, discussing it until it is unanimous. Fourth, we fast. (Smaller children participate in a partial fast, enough so they feel hungry and humble.) Fifth, we kneel in prayer and ask for confirmation of our decision. Usually, the clear, peaceful feeling comes. If not, we start over.

Because we have maintained two separate homes for the past several years and moved back and forth between them (as well as to England for three years), our children have made a rather wide variety of acquaintances and friends. We have been delighted at their opportunities to know children from many cultures, races, and differing situations. We have tried to cultivate in our children a "contribution perspective" that essentially says, "I am blessed to come from a close-knit family and belong to the true church. I am no better than other children, but I do have a responsibility to set an example and to be a 'leader for the right'!"

This last phrase has become a buzzword for us. We tell each other often, "Remember to be a leader for the right," which means to stand firm on decisions already made, to set an example, to do what is right no matter what. Even small children can take pride in being "leaders for the right," without conceit or a "holier than thou" attitude.

As in most responsibility forms, the real key is in setting a good example, creating an understanding of the principles involved, and developing ways of consistent follow-up so that children are always aware of choices and have ability to weigh them carefully and choose the right.

Responsibility for Character
... from sacrifice to chastity

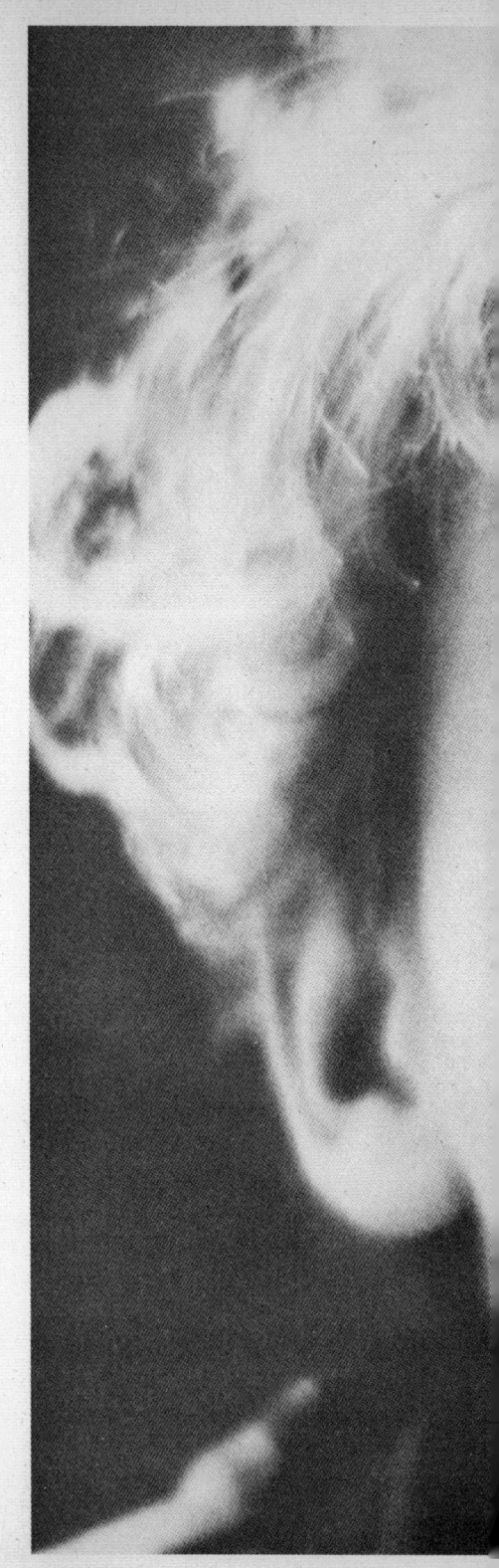

It has been said that, by the time he is fifty, every person has the face he deserves. The same thing could be said of character, only at a much earlier age.

A. Definition and Illustration

It was President David O. McKay who said, "Sow a thought, reap an action; sow an action, reap a habit; sow a habit, reap a character; sow a character, reap an eternal destiny."

One of the intriguing things about this statement is the relationship between habit and character. The objective of this chapter is to assist you in fostering the kinds of habits and procedures in your home that help children to develop strong characters and to realize that the character they build is not something inherited but something developed, something for which they are responsible.

"Now there is a boy with real character," Jim Bullip said to himself as he picked up his morning paper out of the new fallen snow on the porch and watched the paperboy ride away on his bicycle into the predawn blackness.

Jim, unable to sleep that morning, had come downstairs to read before his wife or children awoke. He walked back into the warm kitchen thinking about the paperboy. "That boy has character." Just what did Jim mean by that? Why had that word come to mind? He had met the paperboy just a few days before when he came around to collect the monthly subscription fee, and he had liked him instantly. The boy had an open smile and looked you straight in the eye. He didn't seem to mind being out collecting while most of the other boys his age were playing basketball after school or watching TV at home. Jim knew that the boy's mother was a widow, that they had little money, and that the paper route was only one of two or three jobs the boy held down to help support his mother and four younger sisters.

The boy was probably only a grade or two ahead of Jim's

oldest son, Teddy, who was in fifth grade. Yet he seemed much older than Teddy. Somehow there was more character there.

Was life too soft for Teddy and the other children? Had the parents been so anxious to give them everything that there were no opportunities for them to struggle and grow? A quotation from somewhere came into Jim's mind: "Parents who do too much *for* their children will find they can't do much *with* them."

For the next few days, Jim was especially observant of his children, particularly of Teddy and Jayne, the two oldest. They had a few pressures from school and some household responsibilities that Belva had given them, but not much more than that. Their lives were fairly sheltered, pretty easy. Too easy? Jim wondered.

At Christmas time, Jim's cousin Henry, who ran a large farm in eastern Oregon, came to visit for a day or two. His children were approximately the same ages as Jim's and Belva's, so it was natural to do some observing and a little comparing. There it was again—that hard-to-define but easy-to-see something called character. Henry's children had a lot of it. It wasn't outgoingness; it was something else, something that had to do with self-esteem and a sense of usefulness. These children had to work. They had developed the self-discipline of getting out of a warm bed each morning before dawn to do chores. They probably didn't enjoy it, but the discipline and responsibility of it had produced character in them. Jim couldn't help associating them with the paperboy.

Between Christmas and New Year's, Jim and Belva talked a lot about developing character in their children. They decided to use the New Year as an excuse to turn over a new leaf. They defined several tasks for which the older children could take responsibility. They decided everyone would get out of bed an hour earlier each morning to allow the children time for music practice. They agreed to require each child, when he turned twelve, to earn his own spending money.

They presented these and their other character-building ideas to the children in an exciting presentation.

Implementation was not quite as easy. But gradually and perceptively they noticed some changes. Jim decided once again that the best way to describe the changes was the word *character*. The children seemed to have a brighter look, a little more self-esteem, a certain budding sense of independence.

Perhaps the biggest change was not in the children at all, but in Jim and Belva. As Teddy began to respond to some of the increased challenges, his parents found themselves talking to him and thinking of him more as an adult and less as a child. Priorities and values were actually discussed instead of lectured, and they began to take the time to answer Teddy's questions about chastity and other subjects that they had previously avoided or put off.

What makes certain people extraordinary? What differentiates the virtuoso pianist, the convincing actor, the literary giant? What produces a successful missionary or an outstanding mother? While many factors contribute to the character-building process, there is one common thread in the lives of "great" people that can be singled out and examined: sacrifice!

A friend who is a very successful musician and composer once said during a dinner conversation, "When I was on my mission I received large checks in the mail, the royalties from a TV show I had scored before my mission. My companions always looked at me with amazement. 'Gosh, how would it be,' they would say with envy as I deposited them in my ever-growing bank account. What they failed to realize was that while they were out playing football and Frisbee in high school, I was inside at the piano, practicing. Even now people say to me: 'I'd give anything to be able to play like that!' I have to smile. I'd like to say, 'Anything but ten hours a day for many years of your life!'"

Natural talent is certainly a part of the lives of many out-

standing people, but the real growth in character takes place because of sacrifice.

In talking with people of great character, I have discovered a great many forms of sacrifice. One person felt that her sacrifice was not having a mother as she grew up and learning very young to accept responsibility for her own success. Another said his personal growth began when he sacrificed being with his family and friends, and his education for two years, in exchange for getting up early in freezing cold apartments to study and preach the gospel to people who often slammed the door in his face.

Each of us can think of sacrifices we have made in life that have helped us build character. Even our eleven-year-old can now see how the sacrifice of a little sleep in the morning and a lot of TV watching in the evening can allow her to do the kind of practicing that will make her a musician, and the kind of reading that will expand her vision.

We often become so wrapped up trying to give our children everything possible, every opportunity and every advantage, that it is easy to forget that they need to sacrifice. Sometimes it's tempting to do the paper route when Johnny has so much homework, or an important soccer practice. But we must remember that "sacrifice brings forth the blessings of heaven."

B. Methods

1. *Approaches to building self-esteem in small children.* (To help children develop sufficient self-respect so that they take pride in who and what they are.)

(a) *"Unique You" booklet.* Purchase simple looseleaf or report binders, one for each child, and construction paper. Let the children create the covers by drawing a picture of themselves and putting their names on with glitter. Then make up the following pages:

Hand prints. Using white construction paper, and either water-soluble black ink, a black ink stamp pad, or black tempera paint, have each child make his own hand print. Have him make another hand print on a piece of paper large enough to contain all the children's hand prints. Have each child sign his name by his own hand print.

Foods I like. Have on hand, or have children cut from magazines, a generous supply of small pictures of different foods. Have the children choose their favorite foods and paste the pictures on construction paper. As they cut and paste, emphasize the differences: Mary likes macaroni. Jason likes hot dogs. Jenny likes strawberries.

Things I am especially good at. Help the children make up a page listing their "gifts." You may want to refer to some of the gift-identifying methods in chapter 8.

"Favorites" page. Have each child list his favorite color, favorite TV show, favorite book, and so forth.

Places I've been. Have each child list places he has visited.

Things I might be when I grow up. Have each child list what he would like to do when he grows up.

Keep the books handy and add other pages or review what is already there when you sense a child's need for a boost of self-identity or self-esteem.

(b) *Story: "Everyone Is Special."*

Once there was a king who ordered all his subjects to wear masks just like his face, and robes just like his. After many days of confusion (because no one was able to tell one person from another), the queen said "You may be king, but you have a lot to learn." She explained that people look and act different for a reason.

"What reason?" he asked.

"The best reason in the world," she answered. "If everybody's different, then everybody is special!"

"Do you mean," said the king, "that being the only person who really looks and acts like me makes me special?"

The queen explained that being yourself makes you a *special* person, but you have to work at making yourself the *best* person you can be.

The king decided that he should help people be themselves instead of making rules that they should be someone else. He invited his subjects to come to a party at the castle to celebrate their differences. They all had a great time being themselves. Everybody looked different and they were glad they did. They were glad to be special.

(c) *Game: "What I Like about You."* Gather the whole family on the carpet and place an empty chair in front of and facing the group. Tell the children, "Each of you is different from anyone else, and each of you is very special. There are many things about you that make you special—things that make other people like you. Let's find out what some of those special things are."

Invite one child to sit on the chair in front of the group; then ask the other children to think about that child and what they like about him. Say, "You can each tell _____ what you like about him."

You, the parent, take the first turn by saying something nice about the child, such as, "I like the way Ben shares with everyone," "I think Jessica has a pretty singing voice," "Chris is good at doing puzzles," "Amy has such lovely brown eyes," "Daddy is always smiling," and so forth. Add several compliments to the ones that the children mention. Help each child to feel special. Be sure that you are sincere in the things you say. Be prepared ahead of time with some good, true thoughts about each one. This will help you to know and appreciate each child's own special qualities more.

(d) *Discussion.* Talk with the children about how one must like himself in order to like others: "If you don't like yourself, you'll always be wishing you could be like someone else or do what someone else can do, or you'll wish that you had the things they have. Then you'll stop liking other people." Help them to understand that if they feel good about themselves and the way they look and the things they can do, and if they remember that they are special in their own way, then they won't mind if someone can do something they can't do or has something they don't have, and they can like that person.

Give examples, such as, "If Tom can skip better than you can, you won't mind, because you can throw a ball better than he can," or "If Alice has a new doll and you don't, you won't mind, because you have a new baby brother." Tell them, "If you're happy with the things you have and the things you can do, you will like yourself. Then you'll notice the special things about other people, and you'll like them too."

(e) *The meaning of "unique."* Tell the children that you are going to teach them a brand new word. "The word is *unique*. Can you say that? Say it again. Does anyone know what that word means?"

Explain that *unique* means "one of a kind." If something is unique, there is nothing else exactly like it. Give some examples such as each snowflake, each tree, each kitten. They may be almost alike, but not exactly alike. Something about them is different.

Is there anyone else in the whole world who is *exactly* like you?" (No.) "Then *you* are unique. Let me hear you say, 'I am unique.'" (I am unique.) "What does that mean?" (It means no one else is exactly like me.)

Then tell the children that is what makes them so special and so important. "You are the only one just like you."

2. *Discussion of "character."* (To help children understand "character" and its importance and to prepare children for some of the other methods that follow.)

Build a discussion around the following points:

Remember when we discussed *gifts* and *talents*? (Yes.)

What are some of the gifts each of you has? (The children give examples.)

Do all people have the same gifts? (No. The children give examples.)

Are some people better at some things and others better at other things? (Yes. The children give examples.)

Tonight we are going to talk about a different kind of thing called "character." Character is something *everyone* can have, no matter what his gifts are. Can you think of anything that works like that? (Honesty, obedience, courtesy, dependability, helpfulness, and so forth.)

All those things are part of character. The more of them that you have, the better your character is. Character is the kind of person you really are, deep inside. Now if you don't have some of these character things, can you get them? (Yes.)

How? (By just making up your mind to have them.)

Can anyone help you get them? (Yes—your parents, your brothers and sisters, Heavenly Father.)

Can these people help you if you don't want to have these things? (Not very much.)

You might want to make up your own family's list of what character includes and put it up where it is visible during the month you are concentrating on responsibility for character.

3. *Building self-image in children.* (To ingrain into children's minds the self-image of a strong and righteous character.)

Because of children's strong proclivity to become precisely what they believe you think they are, this method becomes particularly important. It also requires significant mental effort on your part.

Write out a description of the basic character of each child. Be honest in your assessments but be very positive. Start with the strongest character qualities you have observed in him (courage to try new things, honesty, sensitivity, concern for younger children. and so forth). Then proceed to areas where you think he has good *potential*. (Perhaps he shows signs of being a good, steady worker or of being especially dependable.)

Remember that you are looking for *character* traits, not skills or talents. It is hard mental work to carefully analyze the character qualities of each child, but it is also rewarding and enjoyable, particularly if you can do it together as a couple.

After you have itemized both the strongest and potentially strong traits of a child, go on to his weaknesses, but state them positively (such as, Jimmy is working hard at being more tidy; he is trying to gain better control of his temper, and so forth.)

Type or print the completed descriptions (no more than one page per child) and read them through with the children, either all together in a family home evening or individually with each child. Tell the children that you are so proud of each of them and of their character that you wanted to write it all down. Give each child a copy of your character description of them. Keep your own copies in a safe place; read through them periodically, and, as a child improves in an area, change the description from "he's trying hard to . . ." to "he is very good at . . ." Share them with the children regularly.

4. *Family character.* (To help children feel the righteous pride of being part of a family that is collectively committed to certain character traits.)

As you concentrate in your family on the qualities of character, you will realize that virtual perfection is within your grasp on some of those qualities. For example, if you and each child old enough to understand pays a full tithe, then you are perfect in at least the "letter" of that one thing.

Read to the children Matthew 5:48. Ask them if they think they are perfect. (They'll probably say "no.") Then ask them if there are any little things in which they are perfect. Think about it long enough to come up with one or two for each child. One may be "perfect" at brushing his teeth every night, another at practicing each day, or feeding his dog each morning.

Ask the children if there are some things you are perfect at as a family, such as paying tithing, going to church every week, not smoking, not stealing. Make a list. Ask, "What are some things we ought to be perfect at but we sometimes aren't?" (Telling the truth, keeping the family laws, minding our parents, and so forth.) Then pick out one of those things that you all think you can become perfect at. Put it on the "perfect list" in pencil and tell the children you will go over it again with pen when the whole family becomes at least 95 percent perfect at it.

As you make this list visible and talk about it regularly, a kind of family character and code of behavior will emerge. From it, the children will draw strength and commitment for their own forming characters.

5. *Character through tradition and heritage.* (To help children feel a sense of pride in who they are and an accompanying form of self-responsibility.)

(a) "Ancestor Stories." (See chapter 8.) Talk about how the potential for strong character is often inherited, but how it must still be worked at and developed.

(b) *Character-building family traditions.* Most families have traditions they are not even aware of, things they do somewhat regularly on holidays or birthdays or in certain seasons of the year. Write the character-building traditions down on a calendar, according to which month they occur in. As children anticipate these traditions, a character-molding influence is exerted. Such influences *institutionalize* a family and give children a certain security and identity that stiffens their character and helps them to stand firm in their own beliefs even when they are faced with peers who believe and act differently.

Some personal examples of family traditions appear in this chapter's "Family Focal Points."

The existence of positive traditions and family- and ancestor-oriented identity puts a child in a strong character mold and makes it possible for a parent to remind him of a lot of character-related things simply by saying, "Remember who you are!"

6. *Sacrifice.* (To help children learn the meaning of the word and feel its effects.)

(a) *Discussion.* Talk about the word *sacrifice*. What does it mean? Is it good? Explain that the best definition of sacrifice is "Giving up something good in order to have something better." Think of and discuss examples, such as giving up 10 percent of our earnings (tithing) in order to have the blessings the Lord promises; giving up eighteen months of school, sports, and dating in order to have the joy of sharing the gospel on a mission; giving up a Saturday morning to help a widow by mowing her lawn, resulting in a warm feeling of satisfaction inside; giving up a special toy to a poor child in order to make him happy as well as make you happy inside.

(b) *Anonymous toy gift.* At Christmas time particularly, though any time will do, children can learn a great deal about sacrifice by picking one of their nice toys, wrapping it, and leaving it anonymously for a less fortunate child. Afterwards, use your imagination and help your child envision the other child and how very happy the gift has made him.

(c) *Fasting.* When children are baptized, and sometimes a year or two before, they are able to comprehend and benefit from fasting. Start by having them miss only one meal, and discuss where the fast offering goes. Be sure that you discuss how the feeling of giving to someone else is worth more than that one meal you've missed.

Real character comes in children when they realize that it is a responsibility to themselves to rise above themselves. It comes when they discipline themselves to do something they don't really want to do, simply because they know it is right. It ranges from being happy for a sister's good fortune to doing homework and practicing without being told. It is strengthened every time the ten-year-old boy voluntarily shovels the snow from the widow's walk next door or a big sister takes the baby to another room to play when she sees her tired mother's need for help.

A neighbor recently visited a friend's home and noticed five or six bud vases in the kitchen cupboard. Each contained a dead rose. After a few minutes of small talk, my neighbor decided to ask why our friend was keeping the dead roses.

"Oh, I just can't bear to throw them away," she explained. "They are gifts from Kristen's friends. They were all in the same ballet class that tried out for a part in The Nutcracker. Even though each wanted the part desperately, when Kristen won the audition, each of these friends showed her true character and good wishes with a rose." What wise parents behind those lovely children!

Children can do remarkably mature things when we take the time to help them understand how much their actions affect others, and how important it is to be responsible to themselves for their own character.

C. Family Focal Points: Character-building Family Traditions, Early Morning Practice, Personal Chastity Discussions

For many years we have sponsored a Chilean child through a foster parents' program. Her picture hangs on the wall. One evening while we were living in England, we were in the family room, which was separated from the living room by some French doors. It was dark in the living room, and the children remarked that the glass in the French doors was like a mirror—they could see their own images in it.

Then someone turned on the living-room light, the "mirrors" became "windows," and instead of their own reflections, they saw the little Chilean girl's picture. The result was an interesting discussion with the older children about turning the mirrors of our lives into windows, seeing other needs instead of our own, and being part of the solution rather than part of the problem. Our little Chilean child has become a symbol of sacrifice. The children want to give of their means to help her. At Christmas one of them donated a piggy bank and regularly collected donations for Christmas gifts for needy children from other members of the family.

Helping the needy can become a pattern in a family. Patterns are essentially traditions, things we do regularly, look forward to, and feel secure through. Family traditions help children build character in at least two ways: 1. Traditions themselves can be related to unselfishness, to sacrifices, to improvement. 2. The mere existence of traditions institutionalizes a family, gives children a feeling of belonging, and of security in being part of something bigger than themselves. This security is what gives them the inner courage that is a major part of character and of living what they believe.

Entire books have been written on family traditions. We think the best traditions are those that build character, that you have developed yourself, and in some cases that are carry-downs from traditions established by earlier generations of your family.

We try to formalize our traditions. In the same book where we have our ancestor stories (see chapters 6 and 8), we list our traditions by month. Each tradition is illustrated by a picture drawn by one of the children. There are at least two traditions for each month, though some months, like December, have many more. A few examples are:

(a) January—Josh's birthday. We build a huge snowman in the backyard and invite neighbors over to see it and to have birthday cake.

Shawni's birthday. On the nearest Friday when there is a nearly full or full moon, we get up in the middle of the night and go on a mystical, moonlit hike in the snow.

(b) February—valentines. For each of our children, we try to think of one person who probably isn't getting any valentines, perhaps a widow or shut-in. The child makes a special one for that person.

(c) August—Saydi's birthday. In the evening we put her birthday cake in a big pan, light the candles, and float the pan in the lake. When the waves finally carry it in to shore we eat the cake on the beach.

(d) November—Thanksgiving cards. We send these instead of Christmas cards. Each child writes a short poem on gratitude and friendship.

(e) December—a neighborhood Christmas concert. Our

children and others from the neighborhood perform for parents, who pay a nominal fee for seats at the concert. The children all sign a letter to send with the money to needy children.

(f) *Quarterly book review.* Every three months each family member reports in a special family home evening, on the best things he has read that quarter.

Self-control and physical self-discipline have a lot to do with character. Difficult as it is, we get up with the children every weekday morning at six o'clock for music practice. In our case, Mom is the teacher and Dad practices cello while the other children practice their own instruments. Twice a week we combine for ensemble music together. In addition to the music, each child has a household job to do before school.

The title of this chapter is "Responsibility for Character . . . from sacrifice to chastity." We feel that chastity is something that should be discussed in the family, and that should be an important part of a child's orientation as soon as he has been baptized. We try to help each child view his eighth birthday and his baptism as a real "passage" into responsibility. Sometime within the first month after baptism, we have an individual and very special talk with the child about chastity and the "facts of life." Some say this is too early and that children only eight years old are neither interested nor capable of understanding the facts of life. We have found the contrary. They are both interested and capable of understanding. If you put off this discussion, your children will probably hear their first talk of sex from peers rather than from you.

We try to make the discussion very special in several ways:

1. *Anticipation.* We start telling them, even before their baptism, that we are soon going to tell them about one of the most wonderful and beautiful things in the world.

2. *Atmosphere.* We arrange for the child to stay up later

than usual so that he is the only one up with us. Then we either have some refreshments or build a fire in the fireplace to add to the special feeling.

3. *Positive orientation.* The whole discussion is upbeat and positive. The cautions and warnings can come later.

There are two or three good, tastefully illustrated books written to help children understand reproductive facts. We picked our favorite based on its positive, love-and-commitment approach. We let the discussion take as much time as necessary. We try to draw out the child's comments throughout, and we concentrate on three things: (a) how beautiful and wonderful the process is (both sex and the growth of a baby); (b) how great it will be when he is old enough to be married and have children—and how happy we will be to be grandparents; and (c) how the whole thing is so special that it should be shared only with the one special person he or she will marry.

Some children show more interest initially than others, but this first, major discussion opens the way for communication, makes it easier for questions to be asked as they arise, and sets the stage for further in depth discussions that ought to be held every year or so.

Responsibility for Potential
...from homework to foreordination

12

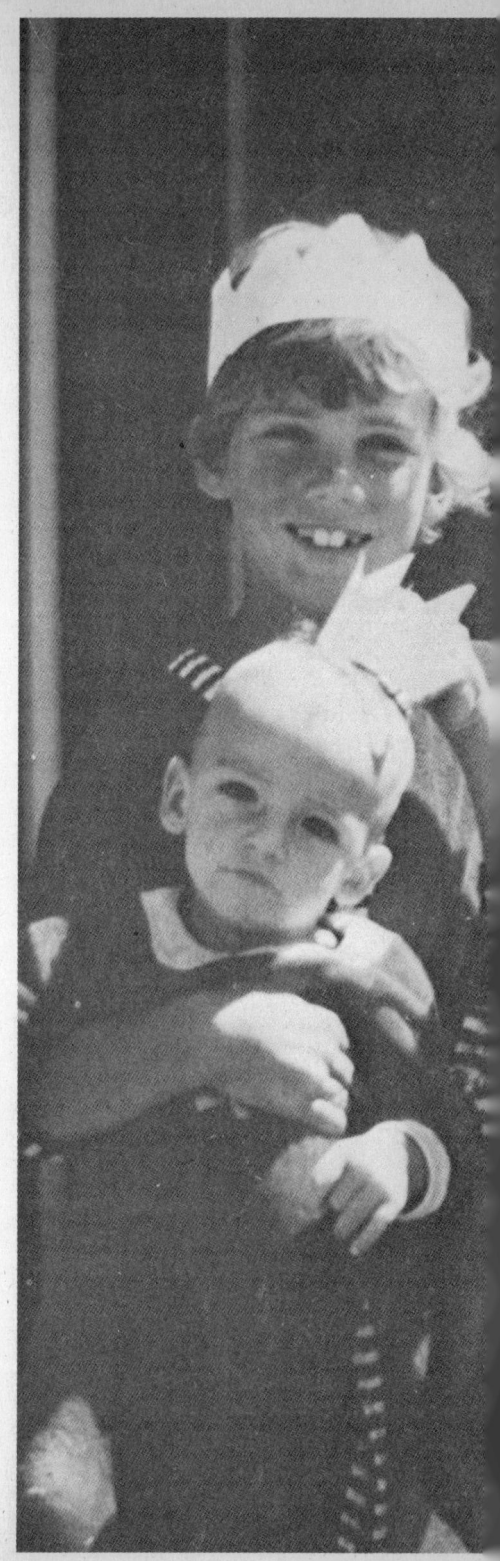

Every person comes into mortality with specific foreordinations. To those who find and fill theirs, there will be great rewards hereafter. To those who neither find nor fill, there will be great embarrassment hereafter.

A. Definition and Illustration

Just as there are two kinds of sins, commission and omission so there are two levels of responsibility. On one level, being responsible means not doing irresponsible things. On a higher level, it means doing all that one can do, becoming all that one can become, developing all that one has.

The highest form of self-discipline is reaching—reaching for the best that is in us, and sometimes even reaching for more than is in us.

People who achieve and succeed, both within themselves and within their world, undergo a certain transition at an early point in their lives, a transition from being an ordinary, average person, reacting to life as it comes day by day, to being a person who designs his own destiny, who comprehends the control he has over his own life, who decides to step out, to lead, to become what God intended him to be and to do his best in all areas.

The objective of this chapter is to help our children begin to make that transition.

When Larry was about nine and a half, he became best friends with Peter, a new next-door neighbor who was a year older than Larry. It was an unfortunate friendship, at least to begin with.

Peter was a particularly lazy boy whose only objective was to escape responsibility and learning of any kind with the least amount of hassle or friction possible. He missed school whenever he could find an excuse, and did poorly when he was there. He was sloppy in both his dress and his language. He had no hobbies or intellecutal interests. His only interest was in baseball. He collected baseball cards. He watched every televised baseball game, and he played everywhere and anywhere he could—even by himself, bouncing a ball off a wall, when he couldn't find anyone else to play with.

In this new friendship, Larry's own already substantial interest in baseball doubled, and his efforts at such things as school, music lessons, and tidyness were greatly reduced. Barbara and Benson Letterman, Larry's parents, were at a loss to know what to do. There was no support from Peter's folks, and the whole situation had developed so fast that they had done little to stop it.

Their first approach at redirecting Larry's attention was a total failure. It was a lecture on how unimportant baseball is compared to studies, books, college, work, and success. Larry responded by telling them that Reggie Jackson made more in a week than they did in a year.

Barbara and Benson retreated, retrenched, and planned their next move. Maybe baseball wasn't the enemy after all; perhaps it was the key to teaching lessons about ability, about goal-striving and potential-reaching, and doing your best—the kind of lessons that could open the door to other things.

The next week they invited Peter over for dinner. After a nice general chat, the discussion took the following direction: "You boys have some real potential in baseball. We've watched you. Your Little League team has won only two games so far. Let's figure out some ways in which you two can improve your own games so that the team can start winning. Let's have a little batting practice starting tonight."

In the days ahead, Benson and Barbara helped both boys set some specific goals: how many hits per game, how many strike outs (for Peter, who was the pitcher), how few walks, how few errors, and so forth. They wrote the goals down and helped the boys create a plan for how to reach them, including how many hours of practice would be needed each night and what kind of practice would produce the necessary results. Benson set aside the time necessary to help, but he only assisted with the boys' goals—the initiative was always theirs. They set up a chart with a check-off system for their practice and circles to be filled in after each game if they reached their goals.

They didn't talk much about schoolwork or music practice or other things for a week or two, and unfortunately, the results showed it. But they did get better at baseball. They began to reach their personal goals each week. They now liked the game even more than before, because in addition to the fun of baseball itself, they had the satisfaction of reaching personal goals.

It was time for phase 2 of the Lettermans' plan. They sat down with Larry after dinner one night and talked about how enjoyable it is to set goals and to work toward and reach them. Baseball, of course, was the example and talking point. Then they asked Larry if he would like to set some goals in other areas as well, not in place of the baseball goals, but along with them. Much to their relief, it worked.

"Yeah," said Larry. "I'm getting tired of doing nothing but baseball."

In the discussion that followed, everyone agreed that baseball is wonderful, but it is not everything. They also agreed that Peter was a good friend, but that he was too wrapped up in baseball and allowed other aspects of his life to suffer. They talked too about what a good idea it is to have goals in several areas so you'll see what you're good at, so that if you get discouraged or disappointed in one area, you can still take pride and do well in another.

The moment was complete when Larry suggested that if he did well in other things, maybe Peter would notice and want to do some of those things himself.

As the Lettermans went to bed that night, they realized that their discussion with Larry—probably a turning point and starting point for the rest of his life—would never have happened if they'd tried to go around baseball and Peter rather than using both of them to teach Larry.

Two mistakes are common in teaching children responsibility for their potential. One is neglecting to expose them to the wondrous possibilities open to them because of their interests and aptitudes. The other is to expose them to so many things that they become overcommitted and have to sacrifice their responsibilities to their families and others.

In one neighborhood where we lived, many of the children seemed so overwhelmed with piano, violin, swimming, and skiing lessons, choir practice, and Boy Scout badges that they had no time for other responsibilities. Their mothers spent most of their time taking them to and from lessons; they also felt so sorry for their busy, overworked children that they were cleaning their rooms for them. They did not dare ask an older child to care for a baby brother, because the older child was so busy "reaching his potential."

In our opinion, either of these two mistakes is as bad as the other.

B. Methods

1. Approaches to help small children grasp the concept of setting and reaching objectives.

(a) Story: "Jason and the Circus Money." Jason was watching television. Between two shows there was a commercial about the circus. On the screen were elephants and dancing bears and clowns. A voice said, "The circus is coming to your town! Don't miss it!"

Jason ran to tell his mother he couldn't miss the circus. His mother said, "Jason, we've just spent a lot of money on your birthday. If you want to go to that circus, you'll have to earn enough money to buy your own ticket."

Jason thought hard about that—so hard that he didn't even watch the rest of the TV show. He looked under all the cushions on the couch and chairs and found two dimes. He asked his mother how much a ticket cost. She said, "Two dollars." "How many dimes is that?" asked Jason. "Twenty," said his mother. "As many as all of your fingers and all of your toes." "I've got two already," Jason said, holding up his dimes. His mother smiled at him and took his hand. "Come with me," she said.

Jason's mother got a large sheet of paper and drew a king-size "20" on it. Then she made a long tube by the side with some marks on it. The paper looked like this:

She colored in two squares in the tube with a red crayon, like this:

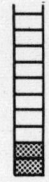

Jason got the idea before she even told him. He said, "Every time I get another dime, I'll color a square until I get up to 20!" "Right," said his mother, "and there are some old soda bottles in the basement that are worth ten cents each."

Jason found three bottles in the basement. He put them in his wagon and pulled them around the corner to the grocery store, where he got three dimes. He colored in three more squares.

"What now, Mom?" Jason asked.

"Can you think of any more ways to earn some more dimes?" she responded.

Jason said, "More soda bottles."

His mother replied, "Sorry, that's all we've got."

Jason said, "Maybe Mr. Johnson next door has some. I'll go see." Mr. Johnson didn't have any old soda bottles, but he did have a backyard that needed cleaning, and he told Jason he would give him two dimes to do it. Jason did it.

Jason kept thinking of things to do. By the end of the week, do you know what his chart looked like? That's right, it was completely filled in—and it was a very good circus!

On the way home from the circus, Jason, who had been thinking very hard, said, "Mom, do you think I could ever earn enough money to buy myself a two-wheeled bike?" "I think so," said his mother, "but it would take a long time."

That night his parents had a long talk—and got a good idea. The next morning Jason's father said, "Jason, I think if you were to raise some tomatoes in the garden this year, you could earn enough to buy a bike. Let's use two dollars of my money to buy some tomato plants. If you take good care of them and sell the tomatoes when they grow, you can get enough money to give me back my two dollars and to buy your very own bike."

All summer Jason watered his plants and pulled the weeds out. When the tomatoes got red, he picked them and put them in a bucket; then he knocked on the neighbors' doors. "Would you like to buy some tomatoes?" he said. "Only a nickel each." Every day more tomatoes were red. Every day Jason sold them. By autumn Jason had sold all the tomatoes. He had enough money to pay his father the two dollars and also to buy one present for himself: a red bike, the same color as those tomatoes.

(b) *Story: "Betsy's Goal."* In your own words tell the following story about Betsy, who was looking forward to her birthday next month and the party she was going to invite all her friends to.

When Betsy's father came home from work, he said he had been transferred in his job, and they would have to move to another town in just one week. Betsy felt very sad, because they would be moving before her birthday, and she wouldn't know anyone in her new school. Who could she invite to her party? Her mother told her that perhaps she could have a goal of making some new friends in time for her birthday party. Betsy decided she would do just that. She decided she wanted to invite ten friends for her birthday party.

The first day in the new town Betsy met a boy her own age while she was waiting for the school bus. "Hi! I'm Betsy," she said. "I just moved here." The little boy was friendly with her. Then she said the same thing to a girl on the bus. By the time she got to school, she already had *two* new friends.

The next day she noticed a boy in the school yard who looked lonely, and she asked him to play on the teeter-totter with her. They became friends, so now she had *three* friends.

The next day she helped a girl tie her shoe. *Four* friends.

The next day it rained, and she shared her umbrella with two children waiting for the bus. *Six* friends.

That evening her grandmother came to visit and brought Betsy a bag of peanuts, which she decided to save and share at school. At recess she shared with several children. She now had *ten* new friends. She invited them all to come to her birthday party on Saturday.

On Saturday morning Betsy decorated the living room with paper streamers and flowers, and she had a wonderful, happy party with all her new friends.

Ask, What was Betsy's goal? (To make some new friends before her birthday.) Did she reach her goal? How long did it take? How did she do it?

Make sure the children understand that Betsy set a goal—decided what she wanted to do, planned how to do it, and worked hard to reach her goal. Ask, Do you think she was happy when she reached her goal?

(c) *Your goal, their goal.* Tell the children that *you* have set a goal. Have one in mind to tell them about. It should be something they can see you working on and something they can see the results of.

Some suggestions are: lose five pounds, make some

kitchen curtains, clean the carpets, learn to bake bread. Choose a goal you can reach. Tell the children what you will do and how you plan to reach your goal. Then show them the chart you will use to record your progress as you work on your goal and to show when you have achieved it.

Draw a circle on a piece of paper and divide it into eight pie-shaped wedges. With colored markers, show how you will fill in a portion of the circle (a different color each time) whenever you work on your goal. Then, when you reach your goal, the circle will be all filled in.

Then say, "Would *you* like to set a goal and work on it and have a goal chart to fill in like this? Think about what you might want for a goal—something good that you really want to do."

If the children have ideas about goals right away, let them suggest them. You might make some suggestions also. If they say something like "learn to ride a bike," say, "That's a good goal, but it will take quite a long time. Let's think of one you can do this week."

Suggested goals for pre-schoolers might include learning to tie their shoes, learning to zip their coat, learning to write their name, sitting quietly at listening time, never hitting others, learning to do a hard puzzle, learning to skip.

(d) *Puppet shows.* You will need simple hand puppets (to represent a boy, a girl, and a mother).

Kneel behind a sofa or large chair and use the back of it as a puppet stage. Each "show" should last only two or three minutes, and you should give explanations of what is happening, where necessary, as well as speak for the characters. The children are better able to follow the story if the character who is speaking moves a little while the other one is held still. Children, with their active imaginations, can easily interpret the movements to be the tying of a shoe, or zipping of a coat, or whatever the dialogue indicates the puppet is doing.

Use the following ideas or make up some of your own that might better fit the goals that your children need.

Puppet Show 1

A boy who will soon be five wants to learn to tie his shoes before he goes to kindergarten. His mother gives him one of his father's old shoes and puts long laces in it. She shows him how to tie the knot, and he practices it over and over until he can do it. Then she shows him how to make the loop and wrap the other lace around and poke it through. This is more difficult, but he keeps trying. Every day he works on his goal until he can finally tie the shoe by himself. He is very happy. He claps his hands and says, "I reached my goal! I reached my goal!" (Of course you just *pretend* to have a shoe.)

Puppet Show 2

A little girl sets a goal to learn to zip her own coat. Every morning when it is time to go to kindergarten, she puts on her coat and her mother shows her how to hold her hands on the zipper and put one side into the other. Each time she works on her goal, she can fill in a little of the circle on her goal chart. Then one day she zips her coat up all by herself without help. Her mother says, "Good for you. Now if you can do it alone just two more times, we can fill in your whole circle." The little girl jumps up and down, claps her hands, and cries, "I reached my goal! I reached my goal!"

Puppet Show 3

A little boy has a hard time sitting quietly at dinner time. He sets a goal to learn to obey that family rule. When it is dinner time, he tries to keep his arms folded for the prayer and not to bother anyone else. He decides not to sit next to his little brother, so he won't be tempted to play with him. When another child screams or acts noisy at the table, he whispers, "Don't—I'm working on my goal." Each day he gets to fill in a little of his goal chart, and then one day his mother doesn't have to remind him even once to sit still or eat his food, so he can fill in *all* of his circle on his goal chart. He claps his hands and cries, "I reached my goal! I reached my goal!"

(e) *Discussion about all the goals the children have already reached.* Let the children tell you about all the things they could not do when they were just *babies* but can do now: turn over, pick things up, drink from a cup, crawl, walk, talk, climb, run, sing, feed themselves, dress themselves, use the toilet, paint pictures, help others. Say, "Maybe you didn't know what a goal was, and you didn't have a goal chart for each thing you learned, but you did *practice* and *try* and *work hard* until you learned to do all those things. Each time you learned to do something new, all by yourself, you were very happy."

Ask the children to each think of one thing they could not do earlier but can do now, and to show that family by acting it out. Help them to choose things that they can demonstrate. You may have to make specific suggestions to some of the children.

2. *Adaptation of methods from previous chapters.*

(a) *Five-facet review.* (See chapter 8.) While holding your monthly review, focus on the potential of each of your children in all five areas. What do you foresee for each of them physically, mentally, socially, emotionally, spiritually? Think of their potential by comparing what they *are* doing with what you think they *could* do.

In these monthly parent-to-parent sessions, best held privately in a quiet restaurant, you will find that specific ideas for how to stimulate potential will come to you. The goal is not to think of ways to push any facet of a child's development faster than is natural and enjoyable; rather, you are looking for ideas as to how you, as parents, can help each child to further appreciate his potential and to feel responsible for being the best he can be.

(b) *Build self-esteem and individual uniqueness confidence.* (See chapter 11.) These ideas are equally important in this chapter, because the more self-esteem children have, the more they will believe it matters what they do and what they become.

(c) *Ancestor stories.* Find any incidents in your or your ancestors' lives that illustrate achieving potential, pulling oneself up by the bootstraps, and similar stories.

(d) *Reinforcement.* Remember that praising the effort is far better than praising only the result. If you watch for and notice when children really make an effort and go beyond themselves, you can then give lavish praise. Reinforce the idea that the strength of the try is what counts—in other words, doing one's best.

3. *Consistent scheduling.* (To give children the discipline of doing certain things in a certain order each day and the security that comes from living in a predictable, ordered environment.)

A home is not an army barracks and should not be run like one. It does, however, pay great dividends to have certain things happen on a dependable, consistent, disciplined basis. This helps children not only in achieving potential but also in building character. As far as possible, breakfast and dinner ought to be served at the same time each day, both preceded by kneeling prayer, and both with all family members present. Responsibilities such as household chores, music practice, and homework should prioritized so that they are accomplished before other things, such as watching television, are permitted.

With children in grade school, homework should always be done before dinner, and certainly before any television watching is permitted.

Fortunately, good habits are as difficult to break as bad ones, and if children develop a pattern of doing a thing at a consistent, predictable time, they will stay with it and greatly increase their chances of reaching their potential in that thing.

Developing potential is a responsibility that begins when we are children, and it never ends. The best way to teach children that it is their responsibility to develop their potential is through our own example. If a child sees a father really trying to improve his tennis game or a mother jogging a few minutes every morning, the child is much more likely to follow suit in terms of developing his own potential. "A picture is worth a thousand words."

4. *Story: "The Drop of Rain that Didn't Fall."* (To help children feel that if they don't do their best, it will affect other people.)

Tell the following story in your own words:

Randy, the raindrop, was supposed to jump out of his fleecy, little gray cloud and fall down to earth to water a rose. But Randy was lazy. He liked the soft little cloud; he was comfortable there. Besides, what difference would it make if he never fell. He was just one little raindrop.

So Randy didn't do his job. He didn't do his best. He didn't fall. Because he didn't fall, the rose didn't grow quite as big or as red as it should have done. Because the rose wasn't quite as big or red, the wedding bouquet it went into didn't look quite as pretty.

Carry this story as far along as seems reasonable to you. Then ask, *Was* it important for the little drop to fall? Is it always important to do our best? If we don't, does it make a difference to others? Give some examples:

(a) A missionary who doesn't do his best (people don't hear the gospel).

(b) A sixth-grader who doesn't do his best (he may not get into college, may not have as good a job, may not be able to take good care of his family.)

(c) An airplane pilot who doesn't do his best.

(d) A ballplayer who doesn't do his best.

(e) A babysitter who doesn't do her best.

(f) A ballet student who doesn't do her best.

In each case, talk about how failure to do one's best affects other people negatively, and how they are affected positively when we *do* do our best. Work the conversation around to the concept of "where much is given, much is expected." Take your time on this part. If you can get this one principle across, the children will feel responsibility for reaching their potential.

5. *"Good, the enemy of best."* (To help children see that their responsibility is not merely to "get by," but to reach their own personal best.)

Put a sign up somewhere in the house that says, "Good, the enemy of best." Don't say anything about it, but make it prominent enough that the children can't help seeing it and asking about it. Put them off just long enough to heighten their interest; then gather them together and talk about how those who are satisfied just to do good never reach—or even discover—their best. Let the children help you think of examples.

6. *Exposure to excellence.* (To help children awaken their latent interests, gifts, talents, and potentials.)

Expose your children to excellence in music, ballet, professional basketball, astronomy, gymnastics—wherever you can find major talent and expertise. If not directly, do so through magazines, books, selected television. Broaden their horizons while you direct them toward excellence. Show them enough variety that they realize the value of finding and being their true selves.

7. *Setting records.* (To assist children in feeling the joy of improving their previous best and in taking the responsibility of continuing to do so.)

Make a chart in which you set up a matrix of simple athletic events opposite the children's names, and let each child establish his own personal "record" for each event. Record their best tries and schedule a time for another try. Tell them what they can do to practice in the meantime. Emphasize only the competition with themselves—never competition with one another.

8. *Coping with shyness.* (To help naturally shy children overcome this potential barrier to their potential.)

Some children fail to realize their potential (or even to glimpse it) because of their tendency to be shy and withdrawn and a related tendency not to try or experiment.

Whole books have been written on this subject, of course, but perhaps the simplest and most reliable way to help grade-school children overcome peer shyness is to arrange to have children from their class visit your child to play at your home, followed by a return visit of your child to their home. For a shy child, there is nothing like having a friend over—to play with his toys, to meet his mom, to eat off his plates. The commonality and familiarity make it easier to talk to each other at school.

The best way is to have your child do the inviting. If he is too shy, engineer an exchange visit yourself (parent-to-parent). The results may not be dramatic or immediate, but the shyness will begin to fade.

One of the most valuable ways for both parent and child to fulfill their potential (and possibly to cut down on the hassle and transportation to and from all kinds of lessons) is for parents to teach their own children. Obviously, few parents are qualified to teach a ten-year-old to play the cello. But each parent has a vast store of knowledge that we should rediscover and pass on to our children. When we run out of knowledge or know-how, we can always resort to books written by experts.

This year, we are studying art with our family. All of our children enjoy art, but I do not have time to drive each one to an art class each week. Therefore, we are using the library to check out books on art and famous artists. Having never studied art, we are discovering a whole new world.

C. Family Focal Points: "Sunday Sessions," Family "Major" and "Minor"

On our mission, we found that next to prayer and true spirituality, the most important tool a missionary can possess is the ability to set and meet appropriate and prayerfully set goals. We used, on our own planning sheets and theirs, a simple procedure of filling in a round circle drawn next to each goal to signify its accomplishment or completion.

Afterward, as we developed and operated a chain of preschools, we found that the same system, on a more basic level, worked well for three- and four-year-olds. They became as excited about coloring in their circles as the missionaries did.

People need progress. Indeed, the objective of eternity is eternal progress. We thrive on positive change.

Since our oldest children were three and four years old, we have held "Sunday sessions." These are nothing more than a quiet time when each family member thinks about the week ahead, sets some goals, and records those goals on his calendar or plan for the week. Little children simply draw a "picture" of two goals, putting a circle by each and drawing lines to the days of the week they intend to work on that goal. A child's completed "Sunday session" chart may look like this.

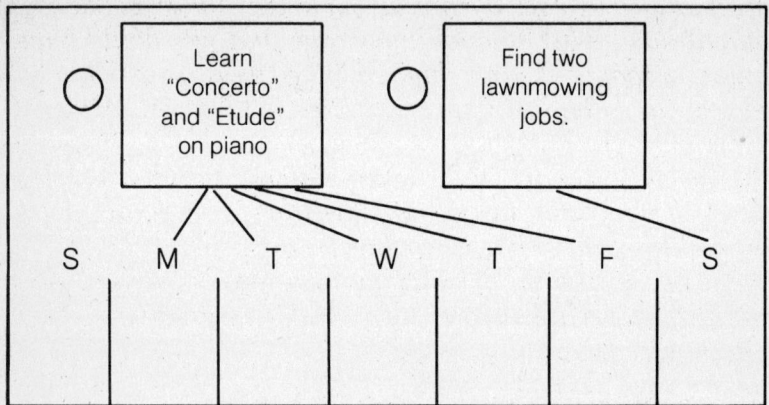

It is important that they understand the difference between a *goal* and a *plan*. For instance, "practicing the piano every day" is not a goal but a plan. The goal may be to learn two new pieces.

One week our four-year-old daughter set goals of learning a new piece on the piano and learning to tie her shoe. She planned to work on the one goal on Monday, Tuesday, and Wednesday, and the other goal the last three days of the week.

In recent years, we have never had to suggest or prompt "Sunday sessions." The children prompt us. They want to do them; they want the short interview with their father where they explain their goals; they want to see their goal diagrams up on the bulletin board; they want to keep track of the days of the week and remember which goal they are working on each day; they want to fill in those circles; they want to bring the completed circles to Dad at the end of the week.

Once children become interested in setting weekly goals, it is easy to find opportunities to counsel them on what their goals might be. Often the other forms of responsibility we hope to help them accept can find their way into one of their goals. Thus, goal setting is not only a method for teaching the responsibility for potential, but a vehicle for teaching self-commitment on other forms of responsibility as well.

In connection with our "Sunday sessions," we have the children write in their journals. Thus they are looking back over the week just passed as well as forward to the week ahead. One helps with the other, and both help with the children's acceptance of responsibility for potential.

As a framework for our objectives, we have a family "major" and "minor" each year, two things that we are concentrating on together during the year as far as our interests and learning are concerned. One year our major was music and our minor was tennis. We brought home library books on great composers, took lessons, listened to records, studied composers; we related everything we could to these areas of emphasis. Another year the major was painting and graphic art and the minor was the Spanish language.

Deciding on specific areas of focus opens whole new worlds to our children, and it gives them some specific areas of concentration for their weekly goals. Over the years our older children have become remarkably adept at setting and reaching goals. They understand that they can, with God's help, accomplish any righteous desire of their hearts.

To symbolize this, I brought home some silver rings from a business trip. I gave each of them a ring and showed them that the rings had no end—that a circle goes on forever. The rings remind them that there is no end to what they can do, that through goals and plans and God's help, they can accomplish any righteous desire of their hearts. Over time the "family rings" have become a symbol of standing firm for what the children know is right.

Feeling the *responsibility for potential* comes gradually for children, but it can and does come. Some of the methods in this chapter can start the ball rolling, and some of the regular, ongoing practices like Sunday sessions can keep it rolling.

The "war stories" that surround music practice seem to go like this: "I begged my mother to let me quit piano and she did. Now I'd give anything if she hadn't." "My mother forced me to practice for so long and so hard that as soon as I could, I dropped it like a hot potato and haven't touched it since." "I hated not being able to watch TV or play with a friend until my practicing was done. My mother used to stand over me with clenched fists, saying, 'Someday you'll thank me for this!' She was right. I'll never be able to thank her enough."

I've never been a person who naturally loved to practice, and I've never had a child like that either. I practiced because I felt I owed it to my parents and sometimes because I had a recital and didn't want to be embarrassed. I think it would have been helpful if someone had taught me that if I didn't develop my musical gifts, I would lose them.

We need to help our children understand what is taught in Matthew 25 in the parable of the talents. We also need to realize that Satan often uses fear to tempt children to give up on their potential. As a youngster I was preoccupied with fear at each performance, in spite of having practiced hundreds of hours on my violin. Only a series of fortunate experiences with music prevented me from quitting.

However, all this theory regarding talents still does not answer the question: How do I get my child to practice? As many of you have done, we tried every reward from stars to Saturday movies, but we were still experiencing uprisings and rebellions. I hated dragging children out of their beds and listening to their complaints.

The turning point came when we decided to turn the responsibility over to them. We worked out a plan that was *agreeable to all. Everyone knew exactly what was expected in regard to time, place, and length of practice; we offered each a pleasant reward (see chapter 8 on paying children for practice), handed him or her an alarm clock, and said, "Good luck!"*

Slowly but surely they became much more consistent in practicing—so much so that we can hardly believe our eyes! As their latent talent began to emerge, we found real joy in talking to them about the wonderful gifts they had been given and their responsibility to develop them.

SECTION IV

RESPONSIBILITY TO OTHERS
(Service)

When responsibility becomes associated with service, it takes on Christlike qualities. To feel responsible to parents and authority figures, and later to self, is obedience and maturity, but to feel responsible to others is love—responsibility of the purest form and the highest dimension.

One of the things that puts the Savior so far above anyone else who has ever lived on this earth is his perfect and total acceptance of responsibility for others. He cares for everyone more than we are able to care for anyone. He loves us all in a selfsacrificing, responsibility-assuming way. When we accept responsibility that is not our obligation, when we take on burdens that should be others', then we begin to develop a Christlike character.

Even the most mature adult finds it difficult to think consistently in terms of responsibility for others, so how can we possibly teach that concept to children? The truth is that they may well be more adept at learning it than we are. They are more flexible, more unaffected by the selfishness and self-centeredness of the world. They are, in many ways, closer to Christ and less weaned away by the weaknesses of mortality. Thus they can feel responsibility for their brothers and sisters. They need only to be pointed in the right direction. The beauty is that, as we point them in that direction, we end up facing the light ourselves!

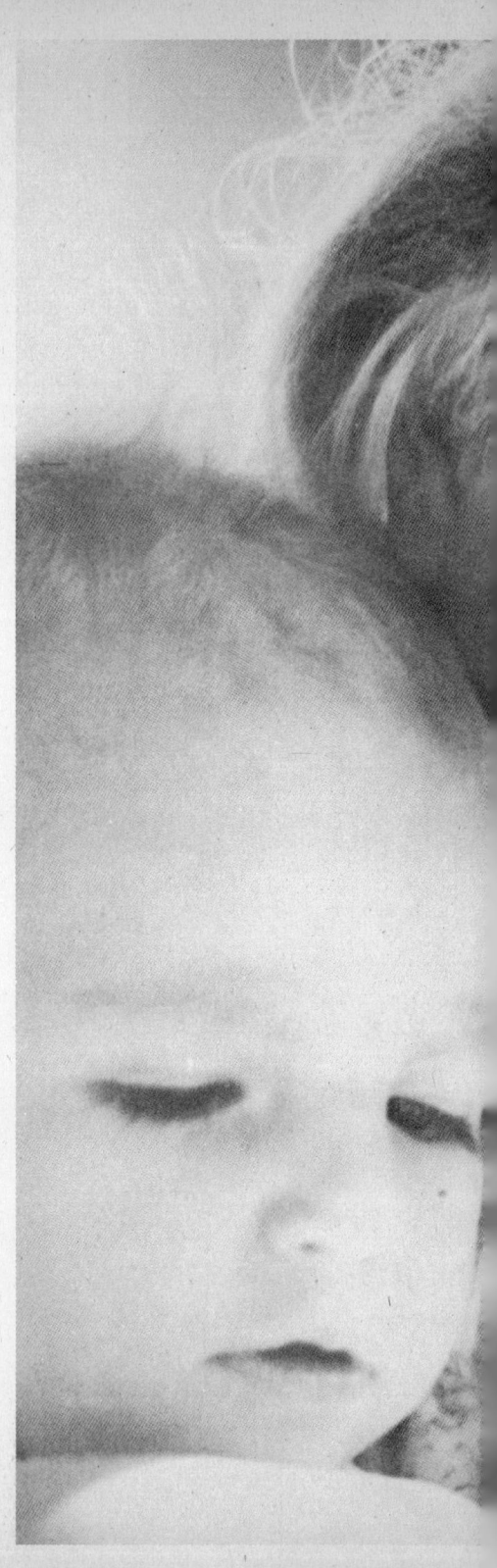

Responsibility for Smaller Children 13
... from tending to teaching

The point at which older children start becoming part of the solution rather than part of the problem is the point at which families move into a higher realm of calmness and order.

The goal of good parents is to turn children into good parents.

A. Definition and Illustration

About the time they turn eight, most children experience strong desires to begin the transition from child to adult. They want to be treated as adults, to have the opportunities of adults; and, while they probably won't admit it, they want some of the *responsibilities* of adults. One of the clearest and most demonstrable ways to separate them from little children is to give them some responsibilities for the smaller children in the family.

The old adage "You don't really learn until you teach" is absolutely true. By molding your older children into teachers for the younger ones, you do three things: (1) lighten *your* load; (2) teach the younger ones more than you could teach them on your own; and (3) bring about the ultimate learning experience for the older children, who learn by teaching.

Todd and Sally had always wanted a large family, and their circumstances were comfortable enough to allow it. They lived in a rural area with lots of space. Todd's salary was adequate to support a large family. Sally bore children easily. They had six children in eight years. And their children were each bright and special.

Just lately, the responsibilities for so many children had really caught up with Todd and Sally. Demands for time and attention often seemed physically impossible. Just sitting at the dinner table and trying to talk all at once to the four who could talk, in between feeding and changing the diapers of the two who were still in them, was a harrowing experience.

They needed help. Six small children for two adults to handle seemed overwhelming.

One night while they were out to dinner, a new and different idea occurred to Todd and Sally. Though they were trying not to think about the kids, the pressure of the six-to-two ratio kept coming up in their conversation.

"You know, if we could just turn one of those kids into an adult, take one away from their side and add one to our side, it would be five to three—not nearly such bad odds." Todd was doing some mental meandering, thinking out loud.

Sally kept the thought going. "Well, Judith is eight. It's been nine months since she was baptized, and she's accountable and responsible for her own actions now. Maybe we ought to recruit her over to our side—tell her that from now on she's on our team and shares the adult responsibilities."

Todd, a stockbroker, became intrigued with the numbers. "Hey, in ten more months, Terry will be eight. If we can recruit him too, we would even up the battle with four to a side!"

What started off as a rambling and only half-serious thought became more important and more feasible as they discussed it.

Later that week, they sat down to discuss the situation with Judith. They made it seem like a graduation. They congratulated Judith for reaching a point of maturity where she could become one of the three "grown-ups" in the family. They told her that she would now be included in lots of new things: she would be included in the special Sunday planning meeting that Mom and Dad always held; she would be able to stay up for an extra half hour each night; she would be able to sit with the grown-ups instead of the children at Thanksgiving dinner and other times with relatives came over; and she would be able to start taking care of the other children more, just as Mom and Dad did.

Judith was thrilled and proud. She took on a slightly different demeanor from that moment; she seemed to stand a little taller, to look a little older.

The next morning at breakfast when things got a little wild, Sally asked Judith to change the baby instead of trying to do it herself. When Billy needed help finding his shoes, Judith did it. When everyone talked at once, Sally told some of them to ask their questions of Judith instead of her. That evening, Todd and Sally, with Judith's help, put the other children to bed and left Judith to babysit while they went out for a while. Actually, they didn't go far, and they came back at least once to peek in the window and see how things were going, but they *did* go out, and they *did* leave Judith in charge.

With quiet looks and warm words, they praised Judith for her new role. They thanked her and let her know honestly and sincerely that she was making their lives happier. They also prodded the children to say thank you to their big sister more often.

It worked. The ratio was five to three. And a few months later it was four to four. But nine *more* months later it was five to four—the children were ahead again.

B. Methods

1. Helping younger siblings get ready for bed or church. (To help small children feel the satisfaction of helping the still smaller ones.)

One of the earliest opportunities for children to help their younger brothers and sisters comes in the clothes-changing area. A four-year-old who can dress himself can also help a two-year-old get dressed. With a lavish amount of praise as their reward, it is amazing how much children enjoy offering and giving this help.

Making it into a race can keep this activity interesting. One evening you might say to your four-year-old son Jason, "Let's time you and see how fast you can get your pajamas on and be back out here in the living room. You'll need to put your clothes away in the drawer, too. Ready, steady, go!"

After the fun of setting and breaking records is established, say, "Okay, Jason, tonight I think you're old enough to try a new kind of record. Let's see how long it takes both you and Jimmy to get your pajamas on. Okay, Jimmy? Jason, you'll have to help Jimmy a lot. Can you do it?"

The praise has to be increased for this double accomplishment. Jason needs to feel not only the satisfaction of getting something done fast, but also of being big enough to help his little brother do it as well. Say things such as, "You know, Jason, I think you got Jimmy ready faster than *I* could have."

Remember to praise Jimmy too, so that he will continue to be cooperative in the joint venture.

2. *The "buddy system."* (To help children feel responsibility at certain times for their younger brothers and sisters, and to keep from losing one of them when you are in a public place.)

In a large family, let the children pair off with each other as buddies so that they stay in twos and don't get split off or lost in public places. In a smaller family, an older child can be assigned to a younger one. In either case, the key is to emphasize the responsibility of the older child in the pair and to give generous praise after the fact for the good job he has done.

3. *Family home evening and other teaching.* (To develop children's teaching skills and to allow them to feel their ability to mold and influence their younger brothers and sisters.)

Most eight- to twelve-year-olds are surprisingly good teachers of smaller children, particularly if there are no adults around to intimidate them. If approached positively, children will respond to an invitation to teach a family home evening and regard it as an honor. In fact, they will often read and prepare the lesson from the manual better than you would have. The teaching techniques and methods they have observed you use will be displayed, along with some new ones of their own. Again, praise after the fact is the key to a repeat performance the next time you ask.

Some children will do fine with you present. Others will do much better with you absent. If your children fit the latter category, try to listen unobserved. Afterward, ask the younger children what they learned, and then praise their older "teacher."

It is not necessary to have a formal setting or a written lesson plan to give children opportunities to teach. Try something like this: "Jared, I've been noticing how much Timmy follows your example. He does everything you do. He really looks up to you. I guess a nine-year-old is pretty big to a four-year-old. I think you can really help me on something, Jared. You see, Timmy just cannot seem to learn to keep his closet straight. His shoes are always left out or just thrown in. If he were in the same room as you, he'd see how neat you are and then do the same. Since he isn't, he doesn't have a good example. I've tried to teach him, but I think you could do it better than I. Would you teach Timmy how to arrange his closet so it's neat and tidy, and would you teach him to keep it that way? Thanks, son, I really appreciate it. It's sure nice to have a boy as big and as helpful as you!"

4. *Premortal role playing.* (To help children feel a deeper sense of responsibility to teach, help, and set an example for their younger siblings.)

Have the children imagine that they are all in the premortal life, all waiting to go to earth. Let them create a dialogue in which they are wondering together who will go first and to which family. Then you role-play an angel who tells them that they will all go to the same family. They are very happy about this, but they wonder even more about the order in which they will be sent to earth.

They decide to make a pact with one another that the ones who go first will promise to take care of the ones who go later, to set a good example for them, to teach them what is right, to help them and watch out for and protect them.

With this basic story outline, the children should be able to embellish it and turn it into a most interesting dialogue. Become involved enough yourself to be sure that a major part of the role-playing has to do with promising to be responsible for one another if they are the older children in the family.

Tell the children that something very much like this may actually have happened, and that the older children must be sure to keep the responsibility that they accepted then.

5. *Paid babysitting.* (To help children feel and accept the same kind of responsibility that they have seen their babysitters accepting.)

Most children have observed, over the years, the responsible position of their babysitters. Babysitters receive instructions from parents and have authority; they are important. Telling a nine- or ten-year-old that, since he has been baptized, he is old enough to babysit, can generate real excitement. Phrase it in a totally positive and complimentary way: "Babysitting is usually only for older children, and it does pay money. Since we have a very responsible child in our family who has been baptized for two years and is growing up so fast, we thought we might let you start babysitting a little earlier than most."

Give clear, simple instructions. Leave a telephone number where you can be reached. If you will not be close by, leave the number of a neighbor with whom you have made previous arrangements.

Pay the child a small hourly wage as soon as you get home, and accompany it with a great deal of praise.

An occasional babysitting experience in which a child feels complete responsibility for his younger brothers and sisters will greatly increase the responsibility he feels for them day to day.

6. *"Simon Says" game and discussion.* (To impress upon older children how much of what they do influences the behavior of their little brothers and sisters.)

Play "Simon Says" with the children. Let the older children be Simon most of the time.

When the game is over, take the older ones aside and discuss what the little children did when no one said "Simon says." Bring up examples of the smaller children following them, in good things as well as bad. Use the word *responsibility* often in your discussion.

7. *Your interaction with older children.* (To dramatize the differences in your family between the younger children and the older "responsibility takers.")

Many parents adopt a particular way of talking to children. It is usually a loving way, involving slower speech and smaller words, perhaps a little patronizing, and sometimes using baby talk. Often we stay with that style of communicating when our children are too old for it.

When speaking with your children who are over eight and who have been given some responsibility for the others, make a conscious, obvious change. Speak to them as you would an adult. Talk at a normal rate, in a normal tone, with normal expression. The difference is often quite noticeable. Children will respond. As in everything, they will live up to your expectation and recognition of their maturity, communicated not by what you say but by how you say it.

8. *"Parenthood training."* (To strengthen children's desire to accept more responsibility for siblings.)

Since you are their parent, one of the most complimentary things you can say to your children is that you think they will someday be good parents.

If and when they balk at the responsibilities you are giving them for their brothers and sisters, remind them that they too will someday be mothers and fathers, and that the things they do for the other children not only help the little children, but help *them* also in getting ready to be good parents themselves.

Obviously, parents can carry this too far and put too much responsibility on children. Sometimes the oldest child in a family is given too much responsibility, the others too little.

9. *"Tutors."* (To cause children to feel responsibility for a younger child for an extended period.)

At the beginning of the month, take an older child aside

and say something like this: "Jerry, there are two or three things that little Stevie really needs help on. Since he looks up to you so much, we thought you might be the one to help him. He needs to learn to keep his room cleaner, and he needs to mind Mom better. We would like to give you a challenge. It's the first of November today. By Thanksgiving let's see if you can help him to be better on both things."

Talk about how Jerry can do it. Discuss the importance of example, as well as how he might remind Stevie. Discuss how he might bring Stevie into his own room and show him proudly how clean it is. Give Jerry a lot of how ideas and then praise him and remind him often as the month passes.

10. *"The greatest big brother of all."* (To help children see Jesus as a big brother and to recognize that they themselves are big brothers or sisters, too.)

On a Sunday or other appropriate day, tell the simple story of Jesus' gifts to us. He gave us a perfect example, taught us how to be happy, and helped people who couldn't help themselves; and most importantly, He died for us. Make a list of at least these four things.

Ask the children if we were with Jesus before we were born. Ask them what He *was* to us then (our big brother) and now (still our big brother). Review again what He has done for us.

Then remind the children that they are big brothers or sisters too. Refer to the list of things Jesus did for us. Ask them which of those things *they* can do for their little brothers and sisters. We won't need to die for them, but we can do all the other things: set an example, teach them, help them with things they can't do, and so forth.

Once children begin to learn to discipline themselves, a wonderful thing happens: they become capable of being responsible for others. This is a necessary and joyous transition for many families.

We discovered the joys of this transition when our oldest daughter was about six. She had been taught using the methods in Teaching Children Joy *as we wrote the book and tried its ideas on her. One day we found her out in the woods beside our house teaching her little brother and sister about the joy of the earth. She didn't know we were listening. In her own sweet way she told them all about the beautiful autumn leaves. She pointed out the joy of the squirrels in the tree, the design in the tree bark, and the sound of the birds, all in a very meaningful and clear manner.*

You never really know how much of what you teach your children is being internalized until you hear it come out again. We felt exhilarated—as though we were watching a baby's first step, only better.

Opportunities should be sought every day to find ways for children to teach. Encourage them to prepare family home evening lessons on a topic of their choice or the prescribed lesson, complete with visual aids. You'll be amazed at their creativity and effectiveness.

Recently I discovered the answer to my own frustration in finding time to sit down with our six-year-old for a violin lesson every day after school. Our older girls, who are at different levels of expertise on their violins, are anxious and natural teachers, and very eager to get their hands on a promising student whom they can mold and train. Of course, the trainee is not always willing, but usually she trots off happily to a back bedroom every day after school for her lesson from an older sister.

C. Family Focal Point: The Age-eight Transition

A remarkable, almost magical change comes over a missionary when he suddenly becomes a senior companion instead of a junior one. One day he is unsure of himself, immature in many ways, dependent on someone else—essentially still an "apprentice missionary." The next day, with a younger missionary in tow, that same young man is self-confident, positive, mature, poised, a leader, an example-setter.

The difference, of course, is responsibility. Simpler forms of peer responsibility can generate similar changes in children.

When our children turn eight, are baptized, and undergo the passage aspects that we have referred to earlier, three rather clear and regular manifestations of their new position begin almost immediately:

1. *Paid babysitting.* In our case, they have been waiting for this opportunity and know that it is not only a chance to earn money, but a sign that they have become part of the adult side of our family.

2. *Family home evening teaching.* We have a particular way of doing this that seems to work especially well for our family. We call it "pass-it-along-teaching." We use it about a third of the time in our family home evenings.

We take our older children (those over the age of eight) and have a separate meeting with them while the smaller children play. We teach the lesson we have prepared in an adult, horizontal-discussion way. Then we assign each of the older ones to teach a part of the lesson to the younger ones. We then convene as a family, with parents serving only to keep things organized and the little ones attentive while the older children teach.

3. *Executive session portion of "Sunday sessions."* As discussed earlier, we devote a portion of each Sunday to planning the coming week. One segment of this, held in the evening, is the adult part. Originally it was just Linda and I, coordinating our own weekly schedules and discussing our objectives for the week ahead. As some of the children got older, we began to include them and to devote some of the time to talking about the smaller children, what their special needs were, and how we could help them. It still surprises us how much insight our older children have regarding their little brothers and sisters and how creative they can be in thinking of ways to assist.

We also sometimes take the older children along for a "five-facet review" of the smaller ones. (See chapter 8.)

Responsibility for Dependability 14
...from commitment to sacrifice

In an adult, dependability is the fruit of true maturity; in a child, it is the seed.

A. Definition and Illustration

There are many shades of meaning for the word *dependability*. It is a quality all of us admire, all of us want in ourselves and in our associates. On its most basic level, it means honesty—doing what you say you will do. On its higher level, it also means saying you will do the *right* things—making commitments and keeping them even when it is not easy and when it requires personal sacrifice.

A very important part of understanding the gospel involves understanding commitments. Christ's is a gospel of covenants, of two-way commitments between him and us. As children learn dependability on the commitment level, they not only become far more pleasant people to be with; they also become persons who are capable of living and benefitting in full from the gospel of Jesus Christ.

By the time Martha Curtis turned eleven, she was an absolute model of dependability. Her mother, Larie, said she would rather leave the baby with Martha than with her husband. Martha followed instructions. She looked around and saw what needed to be done. She kept her mind on what she was doing. She had been that way as long as Larie could remember.

Martha had a twin sister named Marian. Marian was unidentical in every way. Larie called her "the artist" because it was the most complimentary way she could think of to describe Marian's erratic, spontaneous, totally unpredictable, and undependable personality.

When Larie and her husband, Ben, went out, they told Martha to be responsible for Marian, and she was.

As the girls grew older, Marian's unpredictable behavior became less and less amusing and more and more worrisome. She never seemed to get something done when she was asked. She constantly showed up at school without her assignments; she wasn't obstinate or rebellious—she simply forgot. She couldn't keep things in her mind, and she couldn't keep her mind on things. The better Martha got, the worse Marian became.

One weekend Ben and Larie had a surprise visit from Bill and Treena, old school friends. They went out for dinner, and the discussion turned to children. Treena, who hadn't seen the twins for eight years, said, "Are those two girls still the same—Marian a free spirit with her mind going in a hundred different directions, and Martha a model of perfect behavior and orderliness?"

"Is that your description or mine?" Larie asked.

"Well, both, I guess," said Treena, somewhat puzzled. "That's just how I remember them, but come to think of it, that *is* exactly how you used to describe the two of them."

When they got home that night, Larie and Ben started thinking. Apparently they had been reinforcing a particular personality type in each girl since before the twins were three years old. As they talked, they realized that they had never really given Marian much chance to be dependable. They had paid so much attention to her spontaneity and flightiness that she had simply bent further and further in that direction.

There was only one thing to do—start over. Clearly, what they didn't want to do was take away any of Marian's spontaneity; it wasn't really a question of removing anything, just *adding* something.

Larie and Ben went to work on it. They started with very basic forms of dependability, using several methods in this chapter. They moved slowly, not expecting dependability in more than one area at a time. And gradually, Marian began to catch on. She began to see the cause and effect between commitments and results, between priorities and efficiency, between how dependable she was and how much people trusted her.

Larie watched, encouraged, and praised her at every opportunity. At the same time, she gave extra attention to Martha too, used her as an example and helper in teaching Marian certain things, consciously avoiding the "sibling of the prodigal son" problem. Ben and Larie began to realize that certain methods and techniques were helpful in getting Marian to understand and desire dependability, but that praise, reputation, and positive attention were what really brought about and sustained actual changes.

"The youth are so unreliable," groaned the young people's advisers in a ward we once lived in. "We plan parties and activities. We nearly kill ourselves arranging special trips and firesides, and half of them don't even show up. Even when we ask them or commit them to be there, a last-minute homework assignment or even a special TV show will keep them away."

Then I was called to be the Laurel leader. Of the seven girls in my class, two or three would be there on Sunday mornings. Often I would call them when I got home to see if they were sick. Either they would say that they'd had a late night the night before and just couldn't make it, or they would still be in bed—at 1:00 P.M.!

Someone explained to me that these particular girls didn't like each other. Didn't like each other! So what? I was amazed. I had not been a teenager for a dozen years and had no teenagers of my own as a reference point, but I couldn't remember deciding not to go to church because I was tired or because I didn't like someone!

Don't misunderstand me—I know that as teenagers get older they are pressured with scores of responsibilities and become very serious about their grades and about doing well to prepare for college. What is appalling is that these girls would commit to do something, to be somewhere, and then unapologetically not show up. They considered explanations and substitutes unnecessary! Most of these girls had never been taught that their responsibility to others is to be absolutely dependable. Parents of the girls whom I called after

Sunday School to ask about their absence were "afraid" to go wake them up. Often they seemed worried that their teenagers might be offended!

How crucial it is to teach children never to accept a challenge or responsibility without a commitment to carry it through—to do what they say they will do, to be where they say they will be, when they say they will be there.

Dependability affects not only church classes, but also friends, parents, and, later, husband and children. By the time children are the age of the girls in my Young Women class, it is often too late to teach this important area of responsibility.

B. Methods

1. *Integration of the dependability-emphasis into methods previously discussed in other chapters.*

(a) *Ancestor stories.* Look for incidents from your life or your parents' or grandparents' lives that demonstrate reliability. Compose those incidents into children's stories, emphasizing that those qualities of reliability and dependability are genetically and environmentally passed on to you and to them.

(b) *"Sunday sessions."* The actual process of setting weekly goals, as children do in the Sunday-sessions system is a dependability-building activity. As children follow through and accomplish what they committed themselves to the Sunday before, they are developing a sense of reliability to themselves and to others.

By making dependability a topic in the interview portion of the Sunday sessions, you can teach the concept even further. As the children plan their weeks, ask them if they have any assignments, if they have made any arrangements or commitments with or to anyone else. Put any such commitments on their calendars and use them as an opportunity to talk about how important it is to be reliable, to do whatever we've been assigned or have agreed to do.

(c) *Five-facet review*. As you review each child's progress in the "social facet" on a monthly basis, focus your attention (especially during the month you are concentrating on this chapter) on how dependable each child is. Think back over each child's development and try to identify any trends toward or away from dependability. As always, just thinking about it and focusing on it will bring to your minds some ideas for improvement.

(d) *Reinforcement*. As with every form of responsibility, the most effective and useful method of all is to watch for any instance where a child exhibits reliability or dependability and to praise him lavishly.

(e) *Prayer*. Pray with your children for dependability. Let them hear you telling Father in heaven what an important quality it is, and asking Him for it, both for yourself and for them. It will creep into their prayers as well and make them both more blessed with it and more aware of developing it.

2. *The Golden Rule game.* (To help children be empathic and to see the effects of dependability, or the lack of it, on others.)

Make up two signs, each on a sheet of cardboard with a string that can go around your neck so that you wear the sign. Have one sign say *Dependable* and the other say *Undependable*. If both parents are there, each should wear one. If not, an older child may wear one.

Then have the children play the role of someone who is depending on you—a teacher, a friend, a Sunday School leader. You respond to them in consistency with your sign. For example:

A Sunday School teacher (role-played by one of the children) asks you to give a short talk in church the following Sunday. *Dependable* prepares and gives a nice talk. *Undependable* forgets. In the first case the Sunday School teacher is happy and feels good about the meeting. In the second case the teacher has to try to give a talk herself, without preparation, and is unhappy about it.

A friend lends you his baseball glove. You tell him you

will bring it to the game on Friday. *Dependable* remembers; *Undependable* not only forgets the glove—he forgets the game.

A neighbor family is going to be away for the summer and agrees to pay you to cut, water, and care for their lawn while they are away. *Dependable* does it as regularly and as well as if the family were there watching. *Undependable* waits until the lawn is dry before he waters it and until it's up to his ankles before he cuts it.

Add more examples according to your own imagination and your own children's needs. Focus the game on how the one who has given you the responsibility feels when he is let down and how he feels when the responsibility is dependably kept.

3. *Making reliability a family tradition.* (To commit yourselves, as a family and as individuals within a family, to be absolutely reliable and dependable.)

The Golden Rule game and any ancestor stories you may have found illustrating dependability will set the stage for a family commitment to reliability. Discuss the ramifications of being reliable and how it affects others and yourselves. Propose that reliability become a family tradition. Talk about situations in the children's lives where it will apply immediately: school assignments, music practice, and so forth.

Write the word *reliability* on a sign of some kind and put it up in the kitchen or dining room where you eat your evening meal. During the month you spend on this chapter, discuss at dinner anything that has happened that day to any family member that illustrates dependability or that provided an opportunity to demonstrate dependability.

4. *The priorities game.* (To help children think about the relative, long-range importance of certain things and differentiate between things of true importance and those of only momentary significance.)

Prepare in advance on simple three-by-five-inch cards a list, one to a card, of things that differ vastly in terms of their ultimate importance. For example,

(a) A new dress.
(b) How easy or how difficult it is to talk to your parents about important matters.
(c) Being elected to the student council.
(d) Watching your favorite TV show.
(e) Your grades in school.
(f) Learning to love the scriptures.
(g) How kind you are to your brothers and sisters.
(h) How hard you practice your piano.
(i) How many friends you have.
(j) How well you treat your friends.

Pick the items that are timely and relevant to your family's current situation. Color code the *back* of each card with either a yellow, a red, or a blue dot. Put yellow on the back of items that are so important that they can affect whether we will return to live with Heavenly Father (items b, f, g, and j above.) Put a red dot on those items that might affect how happy we will be ten years from now (items e, h, and i). Put a blue dot on those that are either not important at all or that matter for only a short while (items a, c, and d).

Depending on which items you choose and the level of understanding of your children, some might have a dot of one color plus the trace of a second color. For instance, "your grades in school" might have a red dot but also a trace of yellow because reaching our full potential affects our exaltation.

Put the cards, colored dot facing down, on the table and see if the children can arrange them in descending order to the least important. Then turn the cards all over and see if all the yellows are together at the top, followed by the reds, and then the blues. The stage will be set for a good discussion.

5. *Making others your priority.* (To help children connect the concept of dependability to others.)

Children need to understand that dependability is a responsibility to others, that their motivation for becoming dependable should not be merely to improve their own characters and personalities, but to actually help others, to make others more comfortable and more secure.

Go back to the priorities game (method four) and add some cards to the stack, such as, filling church assignments, helping someone in need, keeping promises, and volunteering for service in church and community. Each time dependability and reliability for other people is involved, the card should get a yellow mark and be arranged in the game as a high priority.

6. *The stewardship story.* (To help children realize that being undependable is actually a case of misusing things that don't even belong to them.)

Put the following ideas into your own words:

Once there was a poor young man named Bud. The only thing in the world that he owned was an old car, and it was all broken down and wouldn't run. But Bud was fortunate, for he was hired by a rich farmer. The farmer was kind to him and helped him in many ways. He let the young man sleep in his house and wear some of his clothes. Bud's job was to fix any machinery on the farm that might break down or need fixing. The farmer gave him a truck and all the tools and materials he would need to make repairs. The boy promised the farmer he would work hard and make him proud.

One day as he was driving in the truck, Bud saw a woman whose car had broken down. She was walking along the road, seeking help. Bud had the tools to fix her car, but he was feeling a little tired, so he didn't stop. He didn't even give the woman a ride, because he was going in the opposite direction. Besides, Bud wanted to go right to work on the farm machinery. There was no one there to watch him, though, or to make him work hard, so he didn't do too much. After a while he got tired and bored, so he started working on his own old car instead. After all, it needed fixing, and the tools the farmer had let him use were just right to do the job.

Talk with your children about Bud's lack of dependability to others, to himself, and to the very owner of the truck and tools he was using. Explain that it is the same with each of us when we don't help people. God has given us talents and abilities. When we don't keep our commitments and serve others, we are misusing His things and being undependable to others, to ourselves, and to Him.

7. *Review their "advance decision list."* (To use the commitments that children have made to themselves, to God, and to you as parents as illustrations of the two parts of dependability: making good commitments and keeping them. See "Family focal points," chapter 10, pp. 152-54.)

Praise the children for the correctness of the decisions they have made and tell them how appropriate it is that they have committed themselves to their decisions by writing them down and signing them. Help them see that what they have done by making the list is the first step in dependability. Explain that keeping those commitments is the second step. Discuss how they are doing on each one, and whether they still think the decisions are correct ones. Talk about the strength of each commitment and if the children feel they will be dependable in keeping it.

8. *Joan of Arc story.* (To help children understand that they should be dependable even when their friends and peers are not, and that their example and leadership may be the thing that helps others to be dependable too.)

Paraphrase the story of Joan of Arc, who, in the midst of her battle campaign, was confronted with an enemy fortress that seemed impregnable. Her advisers counseled her to turn back, to forget her commitment to lead her people, to let down those who were depending on her. "The fortress is too strong and too well protected," they claimed.

Joan told them that her choice was to attack and that she herself would lead the charge. Her advisers warned her that no one would follow her into battle.

She said, "I won't be looking back to find out who is following me."

Discuss how commitments and dependability have to stay firm no matter what may happen to us and how those who make commitments have to keep them even if others do not support or assist. Then tell the end of the story: Joan's courage so inspired her army that they followed her into battle, and they fought with such inspiration and nobility that they prevailed.

9. *Your own commitment list.* (To give children the reassurance and example of seeing your own personal commitments.)

In the family focal points section, there are some illustrations of the types of commitments that couples may wish to make to each other and with each other. If you write these commitments down and read them to your children, it will bolster and strengthen their desire both to make and to keep commitments of their own.

10. *Your own marriage and family commitment.* (To help children understand what unconditional commitment is and to give them the security of knowing that you are always totally committed to each other and to them.)

Tell your children the story of your courtship and marriage. Discuss the fact that marriage is a commitment to be partners forever. Tell them how much you depend on each other and how hard you try to be dependable to each other. Point out that the more things they can be dependable in now, the more prepared they will be to be dependable in their own commitment of marriage later on.

C. Family Focal Point: Commitment Lists

People who are absolutely dependable, who do what they say they will, and more; who see what needs doing and do it without specific directives, are rare. I had a business partner once who fit the mold. I never worried about something when he had charge of it. I knew that whatever could be done would be done, and it was a relaxed and reassuring feeling. I have a secretary-assistant now, someone who manages a particular operation for me who is totally dependable. She needs no follow-up or reminders. Whatever I think of, she has thought of it first, and done it. When I give her something to do, or we decide together to take some particular step, I can consider it done as of that moment.

It is wonderful to work with people like this. The only thing more wonderful is to have that kind of dependability within a marriage and family, to have an inner confidence in each other that never fades, even in moments of stress or disagreement.

We are convinced that this kind of "inner kingdom" reliability comes to a family as the parents and children over the age of eight make certain commitments to themselves and to the Lord and other commitments between each other.

As we drove home from the temple one day, we talked about the principle of commitment. The whole gospel is, in a sense, a system of covenants and commitments. The purpose of mortality is to test our ability to make commitments and, without being forced or coerced, to be dependable and reliable in keeping those commitments.

The more we talked about it, the more appealing the concept of commitment became to us. People essentially want to commit themselves to something. They want the direction, security, and peace of mind that commitment brings.

By the time we reached home, we had decided to formalize some of the commitments we had made over the years. The list that emerged looked, in part, like this:

Commitment to *oneness* (sharing everything with each other)

Commitment to *simplicity* (avoiding things unrelated to joy)

Commitment to *seeking* (actively looking for our foreordinations)

Commitment to *prayer* (often and continuous)

Commitment to *service* (looking for it and giving it)

Commitment to *priorities* (to base every decision on them)

Commitment to *Sunday planning* (to live life on yearly, monthly, and weekly goals)

The list represents commitments to each other, to God,

to certain values, to particular ways of behavior, to individual preferences. It has become a part of our identity and our life pattern.

As our children reach the age of accountability, we invite them to join us in certain of our collective commitments and to make others of their own and share them with us. The prerequisite, of course, is a thorough understanding of the meaning of the word *commitment*. For our family's purposes, it is defined as something one has thought about very carefully and decided, as free individuals, to do. A certain unspoken honor system is involved. Children know they should not *sign* a commitment (we do sign them) unless they really intend to keep them in all circumstances.

Much of the dependability we hope to build in our children stems from the commitments they have made. In some cases their commitments relate directly to dependable behavior, such as a commitment to be truthful and a commitment to complete whatever task they are given. But all commitments build dependability as they are kept, because the essence of dependability is compatibility between what one says he will do and what he does.

In addition, family commitment lists are a great teaching method for other forms of responsibility: commitment to obedience, to order, to righteous actions, and so forth.

Responsibility for Contributing 15
... from caring to sharing

The most beautiful of all forms of give-and-take is when one takes the responsibility to give.

A. Definition and Illustration

Some things—and they happen to be world's most valuable things—work in opposition to the natural law of depletion. We have *more* of these to give as we *give more away*: love, testimony, faith, perspective, inner beauty.

The irony of these very special things is that their proper use and management erases the usual distinctions between selfishness and selflessness. If someone wants more love (a selfish phrase) he can obtain it by giving more love (a selfless phrase). If he wants to give stronger faith to someone else (selfless), he has to develop stronger faith for himself (selfish).

The beauty of this concluding chapter is that it fits this same pattern. If we want our children to receive, obtain, and have much care, much concern, much faith, much attention, much recognition—in short, much love—we must help them to take responsibility for contributing those same things to the lives of others. Then the law takes over—the law that says that what they receive will be equal to what they give.

Responsibility for contributing is defined as the need to develop and then to give all of what you have. The reward is that it will all come back to you—and more.

The goal of this chapter is to help you help your children not only feel responsible for what they have, but for contributing it to the world that surrounds them.

Sean was the kind of child who attracts attention and love like a magnet. From the day he was born he was a strikingly beautiful child with thick, blonde curls, pale blue eyes, and the face of a cherub. Life seemed easy for Sean. He walked early, talked early, and made friends so easily that, at three years of age, he seemed always to be surrounded by other children, always the center of attention.

When he started school it was the same. His teachers loved him, and other children followed him around and courted his friendship. He excelled in his classes, and in extracurricular activities, from art to sports, he was always a leader. Yet it was a natural, easy kind of superiority that endeared him to others rather than offended or aroused jealousy.

About the time he turned nine, Sean came to a major decision point in his life. He didn't realize it, but he stood at a fork in the road. One option was to take it easy and let life, which always seemed to work in his favor, take its course. He had shown some leanings toward this direction lately. He was slightly bored with life and with how easy it was, and there were some things, like homework, that he just didn't bother to do. Life wasn't very challenging. The other option for Sean was to start thinking in terms of leadership, to start challenging himself not in a competitive sense, but in a contributing sense.

While Sean was not consciously aware of the two alternatives he was facing, his parents were. They had watched their son closely, knew of his gifts, and realized that much had been given to him and that much must be expected. They knew that the usual challenges of life were not enough for him, and they knew it was essential that he think of himself as one who carried the responsibility of example, of leadership, and of contributing to the world around him.

Rather than trying to explain all this to Sean in theoretical terms, they decided on a more specific, pragmatic approach. One evening they initiated a particularly important dialogue that went something like this:

Dad: "Sean, is there anyone in your class at school who is a real outcast—someone no one talks to or no one plays with?"

Sean: "No. Oh, yes, there is Perry. He's new this year, and

he just doesn't fit in. He's got an accent, he wears weird clothes, and he keeps to himself."

Mom: "Does he keep to himself, Sean, or do other kids just avoid him so he has to be by himself? Think about that for a minute before you answer."

Sean: "Yeah, I think you're right. People do avoid him."

Dad: "Sean, in a way we were kind of hoping you had someone like that in your class. We want to give you a challenge—a challenge to be a real friend to Perry. You know you are a boy that everyone likes. Everyone wants to be your friend. With Perry it is just the opposite—imagine how that would feel."

Mom: "Son, we've talked about this before, but you know you are especially blessed. You're good at many things. Heavenly Father expects you to use those gifts to help other people and to make their lives happier."

Dad: "So that's our challenge to you, Sean, to make Perry happy, to be his good friend. Can you do it?"

Sean: (A long pause, then a smile.) "Sure I can do it."

Mom: "What were you thinking about just then, son?"

Sean: "I was just thinking that if I start being really nice to Perry, I bet the other kids will too."

Dad: "That's just what we've been thinking, Sean. That's quite a responsibility you have."

Sean: "I guess so. You know though, Dad, Perry is a hard guy to like. He's kind of sloppy, and he acts like he doesn't like anyone."

Dad: "Remember what Jesus did when he met people like that?"

Sean: "Loved them?"

Mom: "Loved them, and was kind and friendly to them. He knew that the way they were was *proof* of how much love and friendship they needed."

Sean: "I think I understand."

Sean's prediction was right. As he started being friendly to Perry, other children did too. It took a few days. At first, when Sean chose Perry when they were choosing up for kickball, he got some strange looks and a couple of snickers. And when he sat by Perry on the bus and put his arm around his shoulder while they were walking to the lunchroom, there were a few comments and wisecracks. By the end of the week, though, boys and girls who wanted to be around Sean found themselves also around Perry, and Perry turned out to be not such a bad fellow after all.

Most importantly, the incident set a pattern in Sean's life. With a lot of input from his parents, he began to find that he was happiest when he was contributing or helping. Partly because he liked long words, *contributing* became his favorite. By the time he was ten and a half, Sean was consciously and fairly consistently looking for ways to help people, to fill needs, to give service.

We have always asked our children to care for the unfortunate and watch out for those in need. During Shawni's third-grade year, she became acutely aware of a little girl in her class who was being mistreated and was always misbehaving. Shawni came home almost every night with a horror story about Belinda. "Today she had to stay in the classroom while the rest of us went to the Christmas assembly." "Today she threw up in the lunchroom." "Today she didn't get any treats because she is allergic to candy." "No one will play with Belinda."

We suggested that she make Belinda her special friend, and we'd see if we could help her. Belinda responded to a birthday invitation. By the time she arrived at the party, our whole family could hardly wait to meet the famous (or should we say "infamous") Belinda.

She arrived at the door, obviously excited to be there and a little early. After hearing her first few remarks, I could see that she was nine going on seventeen and extremely hyperactive. She covered every inch of our house within fifteen minutes and had asked every family member at least twelve questions as though she were the inspector in an Agatha Christie play. During the party games she spent most of her time playing with toys she "found" in the back room, broke an arm off one of our daughter's beloved dolls, and took five dollars out of Shawni's "treasure chest." Yet when it was present-opening and refreshment time, she was right at Shawni's side, beaming in the glory of her newfound friendship.

The next day I called one of her teachers and was told, as I had suspected, that she did have some physical problems and was being abused at home. So we persevered. The next time Shawni asked her over to play, Belinda broke several toys and disappeared on one of the children's bikes for half an hour. Shawni and I sat down with her and explained to her our family laws, our real concern for her as a friend, and her need to follow our laws while she was at our house.

She did not become perfect, but she improved. She also sent innumerable notes to Shawni telling her how much she liked her and everything about her. She listed everything from "You are good at handwriting" to "You are my friend."

Shawni learned a great deal from that experience. She learned that when children have problems at school, it usually stems from problems at home or may be attributed to health problems. She learned that the choice of friends should involve not only people who can help us, but people whom we can help. As she saw other children in the class begin to accept Belinda, Shawni also learned some basic principles of leadership.

B. Methods

1. *Methods to help small children understand the concept of service and feel the actual satisfaction of helping another person.*

(a) *Story: "The Sharing Tree."* (This story, from *Teaching Children Joy*, defines some terms and prepares children for other methods.)

"Please don't make me push them any further," little Oakley pleaded. "It's so cold and damp down there, and I keep bumping into rocks." The baby oak tree was about to cry when Oakhurst, the grand old oak standing beside him, explained again, "Now Oakley, my son, soon it will be spring, with hard spring winds, and then summer, with summer storms. Your roots must be strong to hold the rest of you in place. They must be deep in the rich, moist soil to find nourishing food to make your trunk and branches sturdy and healthy. By next year you will have grown so much, you won't believe it!" "Very well," sighed Oakley with a sad but determined grunt. He pushed his roots deeper into the ground, a little further each day, until spring arrived.

One warm, beautiful spring day, Oakley glanced over at his branches and was amazed to see beautiful green buds all over his tips. He thought they were gorgeous, and he was feeling great until one day he started to feel that his beautiful buds were about to burst. "Oh, Oakhurst," he gasped as he looked at his magnificent friend beside him, "my branches, my beautiful branches! They're about to burst and I can't stop them, no matter how hard I try!" "My dear Oakley," smiled the big, calm tree, "stop trying! Instead of losing something, you'll find a pleasant surprise. You must learn that when you let go of something very precious to you, it will be replaced by something better." Because he trusted his kind friend so much, Oakley reluctantly let go. Almost like hundreds of little jack-in-the-boxes, tiny green leaves began to appear all over his branches. "Oh, look at me now!" Oakley cried. "You were right!"

As days passed, Oakley became more and more beautiful. He loved the feeling of the wind rustling through his leaves, but the thing that made him happiest was to watch the lovely family of robins who had built their home in his branches. They were happy there, and that made Oakley happy too. He was so glad that he was strong and sturdy with deep roots and that he was sharing with others the beauty and comfort of his leaves. Before long he noticed little brown seeds beginning to form, which Oakhurst told him were acorns; he was proud of them too.

One day as he was watching the robin children play, he noticed that his leaves were not so green. Some had even begun to turn gold, and one of his acorns fell off, and then another, and then another and another. "Stop!" he screamed. "I need you all to keep me beautiful!" But they continued to fall, and he shouted, "Oakhurst, what is happening? I'm changing color, and my acorns are falling!" "Don't be afraid," said Oakhurst kindly. "Remember what I said to you before. Any time you give up something very special to you, you are giving service, and it will always be replaced by something better. Soon you will lose all your acorns. Many of them will be gathered up by our little friends the squirrels, who will store them for food for the winter so they won't be hungry when all the berries have gone. Some will even find a warm spot in the earth, and then when spring comes, they will sprout roots of their own and begin to grow. And you'll find that you'll turn from green to gorgeous orange and red, and then the weather will turn cold and you'll lose all your leaves." "Lose all my leaves!" shrieked Oakley. "Then I will be ugly and cold and I'll never grow to be so wise and beautiful as *you*." "Ah, you are wrong, my little friend," said the grand old Oakhurst. "That's exactly how I became wise and strong."

At the time, Oakley thought that was all very strange, but as the days passed he began to realize what his friend meant. He saw his acorns drop and his little friends gather them for winter food. His leaves turned a beautiful red, and then, just as Oakhurst had said, they began to drop off. He was sad at first, but when he saw the children rustling through them and having so much fun playing in them, he was glad for the opportunity to share. And when the cold winter came (and Oakley did look a bit ugly some days), he was happy that he had shared himself. He knew that when springtime came again he would be stronger, his roots would be longer, his leaves and branches would be bigger, and he would be better . . . and more like his great friend Oakhurst.

(b) *Story: "Alice Learns about Sharing."*

In mid-December, a new little girl came into Alice's class. She was smaller than Alice and rather thin, but pretty, with large, brown eyes and dark hair. Her dress was too big for her, and though it was clean, it looked old and worn. Her name was Heather. She sat right next to Alice. The two little girls quickly became friends, and after school, Heather asked Alice if she could come to her house to play. They stopped at Alice's house to ask her mother, and then went on to Heather's house.

Alice noticed as they walked along that Heather didn't have any boots or gloves and that her coat was very thin. She held her coat tightly around her because the zipper was broken.

Heather lived in a small gray house. She lived with her grandmother, who was quite old and who looked tired and worried.

Alice said, "Let's play house. What kind of dolls do you have?"

Heather said, "I have only this one doll, but you can use it and you can be the mommy." It was a small rag doll with only one arm and no clothes. Heather said, "I asked my grandmother if I could have a new doll for Christmas, but she said she didn't even have enough money for food, and she couldn't buy a doll."

Alice noticed that Heather didn't have many other toys and that there was only one other dress in her closet. She also noticed that the house was not very warm and that the furniture was old and the curtains were torn.

But Heather was fun to play with, and her grandmother was very nice.

Soon it was time for Alice to go. She said goodbye to Heather and hurried home. She told her mother about her new friend and about her cold house, her old doll, and her thin coat, and that she had no boots or gloves and didn't even have a mother or father. She liked Heather a lot, and she kept thinking and thinking about her.

Then she had an idea. "Mother, I want to give Heather

one of my dolls. She could have Susie—she's still as good as new. And she could have my blue coat. It's too small for me, but it would fit her. And Mother, you know that money I was saving for a bicycle? I can't ride a bike in the winter anyway. I could buy some boots and gloves for Heather. Maybe I could give her one of my dresses too, if you could shorten it a little. I think she would look nice in the yellow one with the little flowers on it."

Her mother said, "Alice, I think that's a wonderful idea. It's only one week till Christmas. We could wrap all the things up in holiday paper and put them in a basket and leave them on Heather's porch on Christmas Eve. I think we should put in a gift for Heather's grandmother too." Then Mother added, "Would you like to invite them to have dinner with us on Christmas day?"

"Oh yes," answered Alice. "And let's not tell who the presents are from."

For the next few days, Alice and her mother shopped for boots and gloves and wrapped gifts. On Christmas Eve, after dark, they went to Heather's house. They quietly set the basket full of presents on the porch, knocked on the door, and then hurried away.

(Pause while the children experience the joy of imagining what happened next.)

When Heather and her grandmother came to Alice's house for dinner the next day, Heather was wearing a warm blue coat and new boots and gloves and holding a beautiful doll tightly in her arms. She said, "Oh, Alice, just see what I got for Christmas—and Grandma got a new sweater." Then Heather took off her coat, and under it she wore a pretty yellow dress with flowers on it.

Alice smiled and smiled. She felt so happy that she could hardly speak. "Oh Heather," she exclaimed, "I'm glad you had such a lovely Christmas!"

(c) *Secret buddies.* Put the names of all family members in a hat and let each child draw one out. The person whose name he draws becomes his secret buddy. No one tells whose name he drew during the week. Each person looks for anonymous good deeds to do for his secret buddy (make his bed, shine his shoes, leave him a treat).

At the end of the week, each person tries to guess who his secret buddy was. Two prizes are given: one for the "secretest" (took most guesses to guess), and one for the "buddiest" (did the most things for his secret buddy).

(d) *Interest table.* Have a certain place in the home, preferably a table or shelf that is out of baby's reach, where family members can share interesting things they discover. The items displayed might be a snail shell, a bird's nest, a picture from a magazine, a new book, a letter from a friend—anything that a family member wants to share with the family.

2. *Adaptation of methods from previous chapters.*

(a) *Five-facet review.* As you think individually about each child each month, ponder his understanding of service and contributing. Look for ways to involve each in service.

(b) *Prayer.* As you pray with the children, particularly in family prayer, ask for opportunities to contribute and give service. *Thank* the Lord for recent contributions you have been able to make.

(c) *Sunday sessions.* At least periodically, help each child make one of his weekly goals a service- or contribution-oriented goal.

(d) *Ancestor stories.* Look for any incident in your parents' or grandparents' lives that is related to contribution—someone who ran for office, who led a cause, who served in a church calling. Tell the story periodically, emphasizing the genetic and environmental heredity that makes you and your children and that ancestor alike.

(e) *Reinforcement.* Positive reinforcement is a great key. When a child thinks in terms of helping others, when he makes any sort of contribution, praise him generously.

3. *Perspective.* (To help children see how blessed they are compared to most other children in the world.)

Sponsoring a needy child in a third-world country is a personal way to acquaint children with their relative blessings. Most sponsorship programs permit and translate correspondence so that your children can ask your sponsored child about his life-style. The Church's Indian Placement Program provides an even more personal way of both helping a child and giving your children new insight to how blessed they are.

As children begin to study geography in school, it is fun to sit down with them and, using a world globe, talk about different parts of the world. Emphasize that all people are Heavenly Father's children, yet many are cold and hungry most of the time. We are so blessed by comparison, and we should be doing all we can to help others. *National Geographic, Smithsonian Magazine,* and similar publications picture other cultures and are helpful in heightening your children's appreciation of the beauties as well as the hardships of those cultures. The pictures and an accompanying discussion will help them realize how many advantages we have, and they will begin to grasp the responsibility that that implies.

4. *The "widow's mite."* (To reiterate that where much is given, much is expected.)

Read or paraphrase the New Testament story of the widow's mite. (Luke 21:1-4.) Ask the children why the rich man was expected to give more than the poor old woman. Ask the children if they are rich. Help them to see that they are rich with friends, rich with the gospel, rich with happiness. Explain that all of us must learn to give of what we have.

Discuss the fact that we are like the rich man—given much and thus expected to give much. Then have the children give examples of what they have been given and of what they can give.

5. *Christmas activities.* (To focus on the Christmas season as a special time for giving.)

(a) *Christmas charity concert.* As discussed in chapter 11, the early part of the holidays is a wonderful time to get the neighborhood together for a Christmas charity concert. The children perform, parents pay admission, and the money goes to needy children.

(b) *Christmas gifts to Jesus.* Discuss with the children the fact that Christmas is Jesus' birthday, and that we ought to give Him presents. Ask them what we could give Jesus—a difficult question, since He already has everything.

Then ask if there is anything we could *do* for Him—something He would do Himself if he were living among us. Guide the discussion to His helping poor and unfortunate people and to the example He set for all. Then decide on one or two family gifts for Jesus—acts of service done during the holidays.

Ask the children if they would each like to give their own individual gift to Jesus. Have them write (or draw) a promise to Him for the New Year ahead: something they will do for Him or for someone else, a way in which they will behave, a difficult commandment they will keep.

Each gift should be private. Put the papers on which the promises are written or drawn into a special box or container. Take the box out every few months, and let each person remind himself of his gift. When the following Christmas comes, each person may share with the rest of the family his gift and how well he has done in giving it.

(c) *Help a needy family.* There are, of course, many ways to assist others at Christmas. Little children understand this kind of service better when it is personal. If possible, locate a family, learn the name, age, and sex of each child, and become involved with your children in selecting or finding special gifts for them.

6. *"What you'll be when you grow up."* (To help children make contributing an important factor in their long-range goals and choices.)

Most children love to speculate about what they will be. Their choices usually are based on different criteria, according to age. Smaller children usually want to be something exciting and adventurous—a policeman, a fireman, an astronaut—or they want to become what father is or what mother is. As they get older, they are more inclined to base their choices on things like status or money. When real maturity and responsibility are introduced into their lives, they may be able to begin thinking of their future in terms of contributing.

When the subject comes up, add a little "rider" question to the discussion. After Jimmy says he wants to be a fireman, ask, "What could you do to help people if you were a fireman?" There is a good and obvious answer, as there is with almost every legitimate career ideal. Help your child see that the first and most important reason for choosing something is that it can *contribute* something to others.

7. *Making gifts of gifts.* (To help children see that the individual gifts and talents they possess can be *given* to others, that the result is happiness for both the giver and the receiver as well as further development of the gifts.)

Gather the children together and tell them that you are going to play an imagination game. On a large sheet of paper, make a list of each child's particular gifts and talents (see chapter 8) in large enough print that everyone can read the list when you hold it up.

Then say, "We are going to use our imaginations and pretend it is the future. We are going to pick one gift that belongs to someone here and imagine the most wonderful use we can think of for that gift—a way that gift could contribute to and bless the lives of others of God's children. Then we will see if anyone can guess which family member we are talking about."

For example, "I can see someone seated at the huge Steinway piano on the stage of Carnegie Hall. The house is packed. It is a benefit concert for the new school that is being built. Dignitaries and philanthropists have paid one hundred dollars a seat to hear the famous young pianist perform," and so forth. (The children raise their hands when they think they know which family member's "contributing-future" is being described.)

Another example: "I can see someone in a laboratory with some test tubes and stacks of note paper. He's trying something. It works! He thinks he has discovered a new approach for fighting cancer. He has spent the past eight years of his life attacking this most perplexing medical problem of all time, and at last it seems to be paying off. In his mind he imagines the thousands of cancer victims who will be saved from an early and tragic death." (Again, the children raise their hands when they know who is being discussed.)

Don't worry about being too extreme or exaggerated in your descriptions of what may happen to each child. Children usually know when they are engaged in imagination, and the higher you imagine them taking their gifts, the more likely it is that they will at least strive for their potential.

8. *Church callings.* (To help children see that church callings are always ways to contribute, and that they come from a source that knows what they can contribute best.)

Explain to the children that it is not *where* you serve but *how* you serve that counts. Develop a family tradition of accepting all church callings and magnifying them into real and lasting contributions.

Discuss some examples of church callings and how each one can be just what we make it: home teacher, bishop, teacher, and so forth. Imagine first an average person in each position who goes through the motions but produces no real results. Then contrast him with someone else who has the same job, and who *magnifies* it and gives real service to people.

C. Family Focal Points: Family Flag and "Secret Service"

We have a family flag. We made it one summer to fly on the Fourth of July below the American flag. When it is not flying for some holiday or special event (which includes birthdays), it hangs on the wall of our family room. This flag is the key symbol in the institutionalization of our family. It looks something like this:

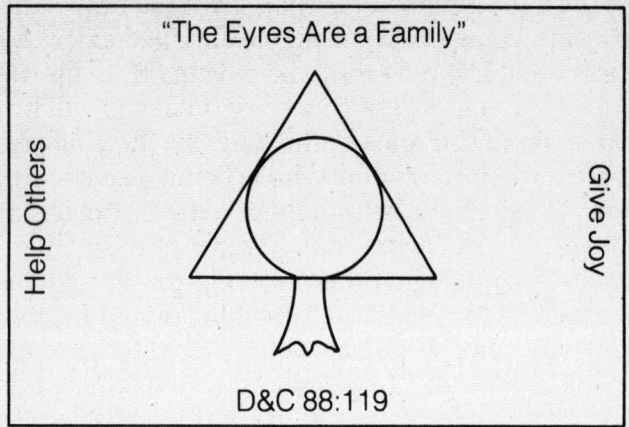

The triangle at the center symbolizes the three things we hold most dear: family, freedom, and faith in Christ. The tree symbol—a round tree with a trunk connecting to spreading roots—represents the children (branches), Linda and me (trunk), and our ancestors (roots), and reminds us that we are each other's first priority and that we have a noble heritage. The five corners and the combined symbols remind us of our five family laws and our five family songs.

Around the border are the title of our main family song ("The Eyres Are a Family," which we composed together several years ago), our family scripture (D&C 88:119), our family motto (Help Others), and family slogan (Give Joy).

Almost everything on the flag, and particularly the motto and the slogan, emphasizes contribution. We try to focus the children's attention on the flag frequently and to ask ourselves, "How are we doing on our motto? On our slogan? What more could we do on each? Who has some suggestions?" Each time we have that discussion, we think of someone to help or someone to whom we could bring a little joy. We feel that the exercise has a subconscious as well as conscious effect on the children, making it more natural for them to view life in a "contribution-opportunity" perspective.

On Sundays, as we are planning the week ahead, one child (on a rotating basis) thinks of a "secret service," an act of service or sharing or a good deed that can be done anonymously for a neighbor or friend, sometimes even for a stranger. These have ranged from a bouquet of flowers for a new move-in neighbor to a major yard clean-up for someone who was out of town.

If the child whose turn it is that week can't think of an appropriate "secret service," we discuss it as a family and come up with something. Then it is written (or drawn) on a piece of paper and takes its place on the wall next to the "Sunday sessions." We decide which day we will do the service, and make a notation on the family monthly calendar that hangs on the same wall.

It is interesting how difficult it is at first for children to think of things to do for others. Their minds tend to function in a self-centered way, and they are infinitely more aware of their own needs than of others' needs. Coming up with a "secret service" each week helps to alter the selfish thought patterns that are so natural to us all.

To further motivate unselfish thinking, we offer the children a "daddy date" or "mommy date" anytime they think of a good service idea that can be done by themselves and one parent.

INDEX

Actions, responsibility for, 86-101
Advance decisions, 152-53, 220
Age of accountability, 12, 78-79
Age-eight transition, 208-9
Ages at which to teach responsibility, 6
"Alice Learns about Sharing," 232-34
Allowing natural consequences, 149-50
Ancestor stories, 68-69, 148, 167, 185, 215 235
Anonymous toy gift, 168
"Aren't we blessed!," 112
Assigned crops, 71-72
Atonement, connecting repentance with, 96-98

Babysitting, paid, 205, 209
"Bathroom chats," 99
Beans, snapping, 63-66
Bed, getting ready for, 202-3
Belinda, the misbehaving visitor, 229-30
"Betsy's Goal," 181-82
Big brother, greatest, 207
Black marks, erasing, 96
Book review, quarterly, 171
Brother: of Jared, 152; greatest big, 207
"Buddy system," 203
Build something together, 71
Building: up, 150-52; self-image, 165-66

Cake in the lake, 170
Calm: programming self to be, 127-28; times, 131-33
Care, share, prayer, 125-27

Character: responsibility for, 158-72; through tradition and heritage, 167-69; -building family traditions, 167-71
Charity, teaching children, 6-7
Chastity, 171-72
"Cheekey and the Laws," 32-34
Child as a variable, 13
Choices: responsibility for, 142-54; of friends, 150-52
Christmas: concerts, 170-71, 236-37; activities, 236-37
Chronicles of Narnia, 96-97
Church: getting ready for, 202-3; callings, 239
Code words, 99-101, 129-30
Coming down from heaven, 121-22
Commission-omission, acts of, 95
Commitment: list, 221-23; marriage and family, 221
Concerts, Christmas, 170-71
Connecting repentance with gratitude and Atonement, 96-98
Conscience-and-consequence game, 91-94
Consistency: as a variable, 14-15; in changing actions, 97-98; in scheduling, 186
Contributing, responsibility for, 226-41
Courtesy of British children, 98

"Daddy" date, 241
Day off, 69
Decisions: and foreordination, 130-31; defining, 145-48; advance, 152-54

Definitions and illustrations: Lucy (obedience), 28-32; the Cuthberts (things), 46-49; the Petersons (work), 62-63; Jason (actions), 86-88; Mark (gifts), 104-6; James (Holy Ghost), 118-20; Mario (choices), 142-45; the Bullips (character), 158-60; Larry and Peter (potential), 176-78; Todd and Sally (smaller children), 200-202; Martha and Marian (dependability), 212-14; Sean (contributing), 226-29
Dependability, responsibility for, 212-23
Dinner: interesting things at, 112-13; -hour calm, 132
Discipline in responsibility, 10, 135-38
Discussions: on decisions, 145; on self-esteem, 163; on character, 164-65; on sacrifice, 167-68; on chastity, 171-72; on older children's influence, 205-6
"Drop of Rain That Didn't Fall," 186-87

Early: bedtime and reading, 113; morning practice, 171
Engineering friendships, 150
Erasing black marks, 96
"Everyone Is Special," 162-63
Example: as a variable, 13-14; begins with parents, 50; to teach care for things, 51-52; in developing potential, 186
Excellence, exposure to, 188
Executive portion of "Sunday sessions," 209
Expectations as a variable, 13
Exposure to excellence, 188

Family focal points: chapters end with, 12-13; should become habits, 19; family laws, 38-42; "trigger words," 39-40; "gunny bag," 54-55, "bed throw," 48-49, 56; "own money," 56-59; peg board, 72-74; "bathroom chats," 99; morning quiet time, 131-32; dinner-hour calm, 132; Sundays, 132-33; priesthood use, 133-34; advance decisions, 152; family council decisions, 153-54; "leader for the right," 154; character-building family traditions, 169-71; early morning practice, 171; personal chastity discussions, 171-72; "Sunday sessions," 189-91; family "major" and "minor," 191; age-eight transition, 208-9; family flag, 239-40; "secret service," 241
Family: laws, 32-42, 51, 89, 100; council, 36-37, 153-54; law chart, 38; bank, 58-59; institution meeting, 67-68; tree, 113-14; experts board, 114; garden, 115; character, 166-67; traditions, 167-71, 217; "major" and "minor," 191; home evening teaching, 203-4, 209
Fasting, 168
"Favorites" page, 162
Fear as motivation, 79-82
Feeling something real, 122
Five-facet review, 108, 114, 185, 216, 235
Follow-through as a variable, 14-15
Foods I like, 162
Foreordination and decisions, 130-31
Friends, choice of, 150-52
Friendships, engineering, 150

Games: conscience-and-consequence, 91-94; code word for super powers, 129-30; "What I Like about You," 163; "Simon Says," 205-6; Golden Rule, 216-17; Priorities, 217-18
Garden with assigned crops, 71-72, 115
Gift: abbreviations, 114-15; anonymous, of toy, 168
Gifts: responsibility for, 104-15; of gifts, 238
Goal(s): their, 54, 182-83; puppet shows on, 183-84; already reached, 184-85
God, responsibility to, 77-82
God-given vs. man-made, 111
Golden Rule game, 216-17
"Good, the enemy of best," 187-88
Gratitude: connecting repentance with, 96-98; -related methods, 111-12; list, 112
Grow up, what children will be when they, 237-38

Habits, bad, 88-89
Hand prints, 161-62
Helping children get ready for bed or church, 202-3

INDEX

Hike, moonlight, 170
Holy Ghost: responsibility for, 118-34; Mary Ann and the, 122-24
Horizon-expanding methods, 112
Horizontal vision, 94-95
How to use book, 18-20

Ideas, implementation of, 135-36
Illustrations and Definitions: *See* Definitions and Illustrations
Implementation of ideas, 135-36
Individual attention, 148
"In-place" tags or outlines, 52
Interaction with older children, 206
Interest table, 235
Interesting things at dinner, 112-13

Jared, brother of, 152
"Jason and the Circus Money," 179-81
Jesus: is reason we repent, 97; picture of, at door, 128; *of Nazareth* (film), 132; is greatest big brother, 207; Christmas gifts for, 237
Joan of Arc story, 220-21
Job auction, Saturday, 70
Joy, teaching children, 6-7
Joyce, young English girl, 41

Law of the harvest, 115
Laws: family 32-37, 89-90; Heavenly Father's, 90; and repentance, 99-100
"Leader for the right," 154
Lessons, parents teach, 189
Lewis, C. S., 96-97
Love: in parenting, 4-5; as motivation, 79-82

Man-made vs. God-given, 111
Mary Ann and the Holy Ghost, 122-24
McKay, David O., 158
Meaning of unique, 164
Method book, 12
Methods sections: description of, 12-13; on obedience, 32-38; on things, 51-54; on work, 66-72; on actions, 89-98; on gifts, 108-13; on Holy Ghost, 121-31; on choices, 145-52; on potential, 179-89; on smaller children, 202-8; on dependability, 215-21; on contributing, 230-39
Mistakes, two kinds of, 95
"Mommy" date, 241
Moonlight hike, 170
Morning quiet time, 131-32
Motivation, 79-82
Music: practice, early morning, 171; parents teach, 189
Musical prodigies, 106-8
Mutual commitments, 37

National Geographic, 236
Natural consequences, 149-50
Nature walk, 108-9
Needy families, helping, 237
New experiences, 113

Obedience in responsibility, 10, 24-42
Objectives, reaching, 179-85
Older children, interaction with, 206
Omission-commission, acts of, 95
Others, responsibility to, 195-96, 218-19
Ownership tags, 52

Paid babysitting, 205, 209
Parable of the Talents, 110-11
Parenthood training, 206
Parenting: thoughts on, 4-7; objectives of, 6; training in, 206
Parents: responsibility to, 23-25; teach own children, 189
Pattern of book, 11-12
Peg board, 72-74
Perspective, 235-36
Philosophy for parenting, 5
Physical events, records in, 109
Places I have been, 162
Positive reinforcement, 90-91
Potential, responsibility for, 176-93
Practicing, payment for, 57
Pratt, Parley P., 119-20
Prayer: for gifts, 112; share, care, 125-27; methods involving, 128-30; answering a, 128-29; in decisions, 148-49; for dependability, 216; commitment to, 222; on contributing, 235
"Pride" sign, 53-54

Priorities: game, 217-18; commitment to, 222
Priority, making others your, 218-19
Prodigies, musical, 106-8
Programming self, 127-28
Publicus Lentulus, 82
Puppet shows: involving decisions, 146-48; on goals, 183-84

Quarterly book review, 171
Questions and discussion, 145

Reaching objectives, 179-85
Reading, early bedtime and, 113
Records, 109, 188
Reinforcement, positive, 90-91, 185, 216, 235
Reliability, 217
Repentance, connecting, with gratitude, 96-98
Responsibility: ages at which to teach, 6; definition of, 10, 23-24; levels of, 10; teaching in sequence, 11-12; to parents—for obedience, 24-42; for things, 44-59; for work, 62-76; to God—for actions, 86-101; for gifts, 104-15; for Holy Ghost, 118-34; to self—for choices, 142-54; for character, 158-72; for potential, 176-93; to others—for smaller children, 200-209; for dependability, 210-23, for contributing 224-41
Rewards, 70-71
Rhyme, three things that, 125-27
Righteous decision reinforcement, 148
Role playing, 35-36, 121-22, 204-5
Role reversal, 37-38
Roses, gift of, after audition, 168-69
Rostropovitch, 107

Sacrifice, 160-61, 167-68
Saturday job auction, 70
Seasons and forms of responsibility, 19
Secret buddies, 234-35
Seeking, 222
Self, responsibility to, 135-38
Self-discipline, 135-38

Self-esteem: in small children, 161-64; and individual uniqueness, 185
Self-image in small children, 165-66
Sequence of teaching responsibility, 10-12
Service: in responsibility, 10, 195-96; commitment to, 222, teaching concept of, 230-35
Setting records, 188
Sex education. *See* Chastity
Share, prayer, care, 125-27
"Sharing Tree," 230-32
Shyness, 188
Silver rings, 191
"Simon Says" game, 205-6
Simplification, 52-53, 222
Smaller children, responsibility for, 200-209
Smiths and Joneses (comparison story), 34-35
Smithsonian Magazine, 236
Snowman for birthday, 170
Stewardship: in responsibility, 10, 77-82; over toys, 109-10; story, 219-20
"Still Small Voice" song, 128
Sunday planning, 222
"Sunday sessions," 189-92, 209, 215, 235
Sundays, 132-33
Super powers, code words for, 129-30

Talents, Parable of the, 110-11
Teaching by older children, 203-8
Thanksgiving cards, 170
Thankful thing, 111-12
Their goal, 54
Things: responsibility for, 44-59; three, that rhyme, 125-27; I am good at, 162; I might be, 162
Three things that rhyme, 125-27
Touch things once, 50
Toy, anonymous gift of, 168
"Trigger words," 39-40
"Tutors," 206-7
Two kinds of mistakes, 95

Unique, meaning of, 164
"Unique you" booklet, 161-62

INDEX

Valentines, 170
Variables in teaching responsibility, 13-15
Verbal codes, 101
Vertical vision, 94-95

Walk, nature, 108-9
Washington National Symphony, 107
"What I Like about You" game, 163
What Manner of Man, 132-33
"When you grow up," 237-38
Which is which, 111

Which would you rather feel, 124-25
Whistle while working, 66-67
"Widow's mite," 236
Work: responsibility for, 62-76; whistle while you, 66-67; teaching small children to, 74-76
"Wrong choice" cards, 91-94

Yamaha School of Music, 106-8
Your goal, their goal, 182-83

TCJ/TCR
Lamplighter Square
1615 Foothill Drive
Salt Lake City, Utah 84108

. . . .

Please send:
- ☐ 1. Additional information on TCR (a monthly curriculum guide for "dinnertime sessions" where parents teach a form of responsibility each month and supplement the academics of public elementary schools).
- ☐ 2. Additional information on TCJ (monthly lesson manuals, tapes, and newsletters for do-it-yourself, in-home "joy schools" for three- and four-year-olds, where mothers rotate as teachers).